SILVER·BURDETT

Making Music with Movement and Dance

PEARSON

Scott
Foresman

scottforesman.com
(800) 552-2259

Editorial Offices: Glenview, Illinois • Parsippany, New Jersey • New York, New York
Sales Offices: Parsippany, New Jersey • Duluth, Georgia • Glenview, Illinois
Coppell, Texas • Ontario, California • Mesa, Arizona

ISBN: 0-382-36621-2

5 6 7 8 9 10 V003 13 12 11 10 09 08 07

Table of Contents

Movement Basics: Skills and Elements

Patterned Movement: Folk Dance, Popular Dance, and Riser Choreography

Creative Movement

Coordinating Authors

Sanna Longden

Sanna Longden is a Contributing Author and Movement Contributing Author for Scott Foresman's *Silver Burdett* MAKING MUSIC K–8 series. She has been working as a world dance author and workshop presenter for Scott Foresman/Silver Burdett Ginn since 1995. Her specialty is folk dance, emphasizing ethnic movement, music, styling, and cultural background.

Ms Longden is a well-known clinician at many pedagogical conferences, including American Orff-Schulwerk Association, Organization of American Kodály Educators, Music Educators National Conference, and other music organization events. She is a sought-after leader for continuing education courses, in-service workshops for K–12 specialists and classroom teachers, and as an artist-in-residence in K–8 schools across the United States.

Ms Longden is coauthor, with Phyllis S. Weikart, of *Cultures and Styling in Folk Dance* (Ypsilanti, MI: High/Scope Press, 1998) and has published articles in many folklore magazines. Her instructional videos with accompanying CDs are sold worldwide.

Wendy Taucher

Wendy Taucher works as a choreographer, director, author, and arts educator. She is a Movement Contributing Author for Scott Foresman's *Silver Burdett* MAKING MUSIC K–8 series.

Ms Taucher's original dance theater works have been favorably reviewed in publications around the world, including *The New Y Times, The Chicago Tribune, The Washington Post, La Repubblica, The Scotsman,* and *The Times of London.* Her work has been seen in venues around the world, including the Edinburgh Festival, Lincoln Center Out-of-Doors, a meadow on Martha's Vineyard, and Slovenian National Television.

Ms Taucher is in her sixteenth year as a Teaching Artist for the Lincoln Center Institute, and is a recipient of the Best Director Award at the One-Act Play Festival in Arezzo, Italy. She earned a Bachelor of Music Education from Northwestern University School of Music in 1976 and studied choreography with the legendar Bessie Schönberg.

Authors

Dr. David N. Connors

Dr. David Connors is Professor of Music and Department Chair at California State University, Los Angeles, California. He is also the Director of the Orff-Schulwerk Certification Program. Dr. Connors holds a Master of Music in Music Education with a minor in dance, and a Doctor of Music Education from the College-Conservatory of Music at the University of Cincinnati. At the University of Cincinnati he studied extensively with the modern dance instructor James Truitte and has performed with the CCM Modern Dance Ensemble.

Dr. Connors has earned Orff-Schulwerk Certification Levels I, II, and III from the University of Cincinnati and he has earned Kodály Certification from Danube Bend University in Esztergom, Hungary. Additionally, he has studied traditional Irish Music and Dance in Dublin, Ireland. Dr. Connors is a Program Author for Scott Foresman's *Silver Burdett* MAKING MUSIC K–8 series and he has published articles for music education journals and for the California State Department of Education.

Dr. Marvelene C. Moore

Dr. Marvelene C. Moore is a Program Author for Scott Foresman's *Silver Burdett* MAKING MUSIC K–8 series. She is Professor of Music Education at the University of Tennessee and was awarded the James A. Cox Professor endowed chair for 2002–2004. She specializes in K–8 classroom music and 3–8 choral music. Dr. Moore's experience with the pedagogical styles of Jacques-Dalcroze, Orff-Schulwerk, and the Kodály Method brings breadth and depth to her teaching of music to young people. She is known internationally as a presenter at the conferences of the International Society for Music Education (ISME), having led sessions in South Korea, South Africa, Sweden, Norway, and Australia, as well as the United States. Dr. Moore currently holds the position of Commissioner, representing the United States on the Commission for Music in Schools and Teacher Education for ISME. Dr. Moore holds a Ph.D. degree from the University of Michigan, Ann Arbor.

Dr. Sandra L. Stauffer

Dr. Sandra Stauffer is Professor of Music Education at Arizona State University, where she teaches both undergraduate and graduate courses. In addition to her current university responsibilities, she teaches as a volunteer in school arts outreach projects and in after-school music programs that serve children in low-income neighborhoods.

Dr. Stauffer is a Program Author for Scott Foresman's *Silver Burdett* MAKING MUSIC K–8 series. As general music specialist she is active as a clinician and consultant for music education workshops and curriculum projects throughout the United States and abroad. Her articles on music listening, composition, and general music have appeared in state and national publications. Dr. Stauffer worked with the composer Morton Subotnick in the development of his acclaimed music composition software series *Making Music* and *Making More Music* has served as the editor of *General Music Today.*

Judith A. Thomas

Judith Thomas is an internationally known Orff-Schulwerk music clinician, author, and professor of music education at many universities in the United States and Canada. She is a Program Author for Scott Foresman's *Silver Burdett* MAKING MUSIC K–8 series. After many years of teaching Orff-Schulwerk at the elementary level and as district Arts Coordinator in Upper Nyack, New York, she continues to teach Orff-Schulwerk Certification classes.

Ms Thomas is co-author with Susan Katz of their newest book, *Word in Play: Language, Music and Movement in the Classroom* was released in 2004, published by Brookes Publishers of Baltimore. She has also made contributions to the American editions of the three volumes of *Music for Children* (Schott).

Ms Thomas is an honorary member of the American Orff-Schulwerk Association, having served as President and Conference Chairperson. She holds the Master of Music Degree in piano from the University of Illinois, and a Special Certificate from the Orff Institute in Salzburg, Austria, where she has co-directed and taught summer workshops.

Enhance your music curriculum through movement and dance!

Feel the beat! Move with rhythm! Dance! Enjoy! MAKING MUSIC WITH MOVEMENT AND DANCE encourages active music making. It provides students with rich and varied movement and dance experiences that enhance their musical knowledge, skills, and appreciation.

MAKING MUSIC WITH MOVEMENT AND DANCE complements the lessons in Silver Burdett MAKING MUSIC, Grades 1–8. It provides suggestions for enhancing the music curriculum through movement and dance while presenting lessons designed to be easily lifted off the page. The wide variety of musical recordings, all drawn from the Silver Burdett MAKING MUSIC series Audio CDs, provide the accompaniment for the movement and dance experiences. The lessons can quickly and easily be used for large and small group activities in music or physical education classes.

Divided into three sections, MAKING MUSIC WITH MOVEMENT AND DANCE has an easy-to-follow, consistent organization that mirrors the Silver Burdett MAKING MUSIC series. Teachers will be familiar with features such as the Lesson at a Glance box and the three-step lesson plan. To ensure an effective skill focus, each lesson also clearly identifies National Standards for Dance and Physical Education.

Making Music with Movement and Dance

- Easy-to-follow guide for movement and dance activities

- Spiral-bound with a hard-back book cover so it stands up easily on a music or keyboard stand

- Divided into 3 sections for easy planning—Movement Basics, Patterned Movement, Creative Movement

- Supports the National Dance and Physical Education Standards

- Provides developmentally appropriate learning experiences for large and small groups

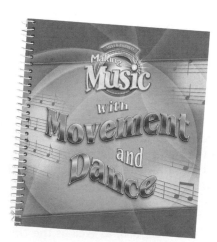

See for Yourself

This Sampler Book includes a comprehensive overview of MAKING MUSIC WITH MOVEMENT AND DANCE.

- Lessons from each of the 3 sections

- Brief explanation of the section at point of use

- Three-step lessons: 1) Prepare, 2) Take Action, 3) Reflect

Section 1 ••

Movement Basics

- Demonstrates the consistent sequence, upbeat approach, detailed movement techniques, and variety of musical selections offered in the complete MAKING MUSIC WITH MOVEMENT AND DANCE

- Provides a comprehensive overview of the design of this section—the sequence, skill focus, and National Dance and Physical Education Standards in MAKING MUSIC WITH MOVEMENT AND DANCE

Section 2 ••

Patterned Movement

- Includes folk dances; patterned, creative, improvised, and choreographed dances; traditional dances; and riser choreography

- Offers a variety of movement skills, formations, cultures, and historical contexts, including dances from specific time periods in the United States

Section 3 ••

Creative Movement

- Applies techniques and skills that students developed in Movement Basics as the instruments with which they create choreography

- Ensures that students exaggerate and abstract movement, making a clear distinction between normal everyday movement and creative dance movement

Movement Basics

Movement Basics—a Sequence of Skills and Elements

Movement Basics: Skills and Elements provides a sound base for building specific technical movement skills through playful yet detailed classroom management techniques. Movement classroom management techniques are built into each lesson to help the teacher convey instructions without the aid of paper, pens, books, or the chalkboard. The instructional sequence of physical activities begins with an icebreaker that encourages use of the full body. The sequence progresses through axial moves, changing levels, rhythm and isolations, basic traveling steps, balance, leaping and landing, and putting the Movement Glossary on its feet. In all cases, students are challenged to keep moving and teachers are assisted by a well-designed technique sequence, variety in music, and activities created within the theory of disciplined fun.

The sequence of movement techniques is identical in grades 1 though 8. It has a sound base in standard dance practice. The movement skills and elements are presented in age-appropriate physical actions, using coordination skills and listening skills that are suitable to students at a particular grade level.

Lessons are designed to be quickly and easily lifted off the page, providing simple sets of movements in which the students participate. Teachers who are experienced in dance instruction will appreciate the logical technical progression. Teachers who are new to dance and movement instruction will find that the format allows students to self-generate the specific actions necessary in each activity. The wide variety of musical accompaniments, all drawn from the *Silver Burdett* MAKING MUSIC series recordings, provide an enjoyable and challenging environment in which students build movement skills.

The Movement Basics section in this Sampler Book demonstrates the user-friendly sequence concept, the upbeat approach, detailed movement techniques, and the variety of musical selections offered in MAKING MUSIC WITH MOVEMENT AND DANCE.

The Movement Basics lessons in this Sampler Book were chosen to provide a comprehensive overview of the design of this section; they mirror the sequence, skill focus, and the *National Standards for Arts in Education: Dance* and the *National Standards for Physical Education* that are covered in MAKING MUSIC WITH MOVEMENT AND DANCE.

1 Wiggles and Giggles

LESSON AT A GLANCE

Movement Skill Objective Demonstrate awareness that the entire body is a dancer's instrument

K–4 Dance Standard 1g Demonstrate kinesthetic awareness, concentration, and focus in performing movement skills

Physical Education Standard 1 Demonstrate competency in motor skills needed to perform a variety of physical activities

MATERIALS

• *Quintet for Piano and Strings in A Major, "Trout," Movement 3, Scherzo (excerpt)* Teachers' Edition, Gr. 1, p. 179

DANCE COUNT SEQUENCE

Section	Music Cue	Count
Section A	Fast violin	4 sets of 4 + 2
Section B	Fast violin	6 sets of 4
Section C	Piano with violin chase	4 sets of 4
Section D	Piano violin pulse	5 sets of 4 + 2
Section E	Fast violin	6 sets of 4

DANCE NOTE

Count in sets of four beats (except where 2 counts are indicated) in time with the music, for example: 1-2-3-4, 2-2-3-4, 3-2-3-4, and so on.

1 Prepare

Warm Up

Standing in their own personal space, have the children wiggle all parts of their bodies except their feet. Repeat the same action with the children sitting, lying on their backs, or on their tummies.

SAY Pretend that your feet are glued to the floor but make sure to wiggle everything else.

2 Take Action

Formation

Have the children stand in a circle or in rows facing you. Play the recording of *Quintet for Piano and Strings in A Major, "Trout," Movement 3, Scherzo (excerpt)* **CD 5-46** and have the children move as follows.

Section A

As the music begins, have the children throw laughing movements through their arms and create wiggly motions.

SAY Throw the laughs in your arms out to the walls, floor, or ceiling but make no sound.

Section B

Have children wiggle down to the floor and back up three times, using four counts to wiggle down and four counts to wiggle back up.

ASK Can you wiggle and count to four at the same time? (Allow several children to demonstrate.)

Section C

Have the children create laughing moves with only the head, neck, back, tummy, and bottom.

SAY Hold yours arms and feet still and move everything else. Make sure your movements feel like laughing.

Section D

Have the children laugh in slow motion, using their entire bodies. Children can use their legs to laugh, but should remain **in place.**

ASK Can you move slowly while the music moves fast? (Allow children to demonstrate.)

Section E

Have the children repeat two or three laughing moves over and over until the music stops and then freeze in a laughing position.

SAY Repeat a few of your laughing moves. Let your muscles help you remember. When the music ends, freeze in the middle of a laugh.

Play the music and have the children perform their giggle-wiggle sequences several times. Observe the extent to which they use their bodies appropriately for each section of the music. Determine whether they are demonstrating awareness of their bodies moving in space and time.

3 Reflect

Cool Down

As children calmly stand in neutral position, have them stretch their arms to the ceiling and hold for a moment, then lower their arms. Repeat the arm stretching movement, this time wiggling their fingers slowly at the top of the stretch. Stretch a third time and have them wiggle both arms gently at the top. Repeat the arm stretch one last time and have children gently wiggle the neck, holding the arms still.

SAY Breathe deeply and concentrate on making slow and gentle movements.

---

8 Airborne Action

LESSON AT A GLANCE

Movement Skill Objective Jump and leap with clean preparation and smooth landings

K–4 Dance Standard 1b Accurately demonstrate basic locomotor movements (such as hops, jumps, leaps)

Physical Education Standard 2 Demonstrate understanding of movement concepts and principles as they apply to the learning and performance of physical activities

MATERIALS

• *Washington Post March*
Teachers' Edition, Gr. 1, p. 175   **CD 5-36**

DANCE NOTE

Count in sets of eight.

1 Prepare

Warm Up

Working in silence, have the children experiment with the difference between a **jump** (take off from two feet and land on two feet) and a **leap** (take off from one foot and land on the other).

SAY Good landings are quiet. It shows that you are bending your knees when you land.

2 Take Action

Getting Airborne with Music

Set the CD player to auto repeat and play the recording of the *Washington Post March* **CD 5-36.** Remaining stationary, children count the beat in sets of 8. Have them move their arms slowly for counts one through six. On count seven, **bend** the knees and draw the arms close to the body. On count eight, jump as high as they can, reaching their arms as high as possible. Land on count one and repeat.

Using the same count sequence, have the children walk around the room, leaping from one foot to the other on counts seven and eight.

ASK How high can you leap on counts seven and eight? (Children show you how high they can leap.)

Turn off the music.

3 Reflect

Cool Down

Standing in neutral, have the children roll their heads down, relaxing their arms and keeping their knees straight. Hang for a few seconds, then go into a squat and rest for a few seconds. Lower onto the back, lift the legs and shake them gently in the air. Recover slowly into neutral.

SAY Relax all the muscles and turn your legs into wiggly noodles.

2 Stretch, Bend, and Twist

LESSON AT A GLANCE

Movement Skill Objective Perform a movement sequence using axial stretches, bends, and twists

K–4 Dance Standard 1a Accurately demonstrate nonlocomotor/axial movement

Physical Education Standard 2 Demonstrate understanding of movement concepts and strategies as they apply to the learning and performance of physical activities

MATERIALS
- *Yertle the Turtle*
  Teacher's Edition, Gr. 2, p. 368 **CD 13-27**

DANCE COUNT SEQUENCE

Section	Lyric or Music Cue	Count
Intro	*Yertle, the turtle*	Stand still
Section A	*On a far island*	4 sets of 8
Section B	Trumpets	4 sets of 8
Section C	*With a*	4 sets of 8
Section D	Trumpets	2 sets of 8
Section E	Bass guitar	6 sets of 8
	Then down from below	
Section F	Trumpets and bass guitar	2 sets of 8
	Yertle…Yertle, the turtle	
Section G	Instrumental	8 sets of 8
Coda (fade out)	Instrumental	1 set of 8

1 Prepare

Warm Up

In a **grid with windows formation**, have the children lie on their backs with their eyes closed. Have them move as if their bodies were rubber bands being stretched and slowly released (not snapped).

Repeat this action a number of times, starting in different positions, such as sitting, kneeling, and standing.

2 Take Action

Play the recording of *Yertle the Turtle* **CD 13-27** and have the children move as follows.

Section A

Children stand with feet together and **parallel**. They roll down, head first, into a supported squat position. Perform this sequence two times, using 8 counts to roll down and 8 to roll back up.

SAY Start the roll from the top of your head, keep your legs straight and your knees soft; do not lock your knees.

Sections B and C

Children **stretch** their arms straight up and count 1-2-3-4-5-6-7-8. For the second set of 8 they hold their arms above the head, **bend** forward at the waist, and slide hands down thighs to support a **flat back**. For the third set of 8 rewind the motion and end by standing straight up with arms above their heads. For the fourth set of 8, lower the arms slowly to the sides without bending the elbows. Repeat the entire sequence for Section C.

Sections D and E

Children **contract** their torsos to make a curved shape and count 1-2-3-4. Release into the opposite **arch** shape and count 5-6-7-8. Perform the sequence eight times.

SAY Make sure to bend your knees and keep your heels on the floor.

Section F

Children open feet in wide **second position** and reach with the left arm over the head toward the right in a side bend and count 1-2-3-4. **Recover** for four counts. Repeat the 8-count movement on the other side.

SAY Reach the top of your head toward the wall.

Section G

Feet should be parallel. Children slowly turn their heads as far around to the right as they can for 8 counts. Take the next 8 counts to recover to neutral. Repeat the moves to the left side, to the right again, and to the left again. After turning the head on each side, add an arm stretch to the head twist. Use the left arm when the head turns to the right, the right arm when the head turns to the left.

SAY Move really slowly and steadily. Keep your feet glued to the floor.

Coda

Children rock back and forth, or side to side, from foot to foot, without traveling. As the music ends each student should become a *Yertle the Turtle* statue.

SAY Keep your knees soft and let your arms swing.

As the statues appear and the music is ended, say *Hello Yertles*.

3 Reflect

Cool Down

Standing in neutral, ask the children to close their eyes and remember how the rubber band image made their muscles feel. Keeping eyes closed, ask them to stretch the rubber band one more time in slow motion and allow it to snap.

SAY Move in slow motion and let your imagination tell you how your rubber band will move when it is snapped.

Grade 2

LESSON 4 — Stop and Go

LESSON AT A GLANCE

Movement Skill Objective Experience the difference between stationary and locomotor movement

K–4 Dance Standard 1h Attentively observe and accurately describe the action (such as skip, gallop) and movement elements (such as level, directions) in a brief movement study

Physical Education Standard 1 Demonstrate competency in motor skills needed to perform a variety of physical activities

MATERIALS
- *Baby Elephant Walk*
  Teachers' Edition, Gr. 2, p. 163   **CD 6-19**

DANCE COUNT SEQUENCE

Section	Music Cue	Count
Section A	Organ/flute solo	Pickup, then 8 counts
Section B	Introduction: rhythm section	3 sets of 8
Section C1	Verse: clarinet	6 sets of 8
Section D1	Interlude: baritone sax	2 sets of 8
Section C2	Verse: piccolos & glocks	6 sets of 8
Section E1	Bridge: muted brass, sax solo	6 sets of 8
Section E2	Bridge: muted brass, flute solo	6 sets of 8
Section D1	Interlude: baritone sax	2 sets of 8
Section C3	Verse: clarinet, piccolos	6 sets of 8
Coda	*Ritardando*	No counting

1 Prepare

Warm Up

Children begin seated in their own **home spots.** Working in silence, each child creates three different ways to perform locomotor movements without standing.

SAY Keep your own space as you travel. Be aware of the other movers.

2 Take Action

Formation

Home spots and **individual pathways.**

Creating Movements

Working in silence and remaining stationary, have children slowly morph from themselves into baby elephants and then into human babies. Repeat the process a number of times.

SAY Discover different baby elephant shapes and different human baby shapes.

Continuing in silence, ask each child to travel like a baby elephant.

SAY Invent your own baby elephant walk.

ASK How many different ways can you think of to show the elephant's trunk? (Invite experimentation and sharing.)

Repeat the same traveling-in-silence activity, but do it as human babies, instead of elephants.

SAY Babies travel in lots of different ways. They are creative.

Stop and Go Dance

Have the children practice and perform their baby elephant and human baby dances, using the Dance Count Sequence shown in Lesson-at-a-Glance and the movement suggestions below. Develop visual cues to signal the children when to remain stationary, when to travel like baby elephants, and when to travel like human babies.

Play the recording of Henry Mancini's *Baby Elephant Walk* **CD 6-19** and have the children move with the music.

- **Section A**—Remain frozen.
- **Section B**—Remaining stationary, morph into baby elephants.
- **Section C1**—Travel as baby elephants on individual pathways.
- **Section D1**—Stationary, morph into human babies.
- **Section C2**—Travel as human babies on individual pathways.
- **Section E1**—Stationary, baby elephant moves.
- **Section E2**—Stationary, human baby moves.
- **Section D1**—Stationary, morph into baby elephants
- **Section C3**—Travel as baby elephants on individual pathways.
- **Coda**—Stationary, morph into human babies and freeze.

3 Reflect

Cool Down

Begin by standing in home spots. Each child walks slowly on his or her own pathway for sixteen counts, getting lower and slower. By count sixteen, all children should be on the floor. For the next sixteen counts, children remain stationary as they slowly stand, ending in neutral.

SAY Use your muscles carefully as you go up and down. Keep the movements smooth.

LESSON

1 I See You Laughing!

LESSON AT A GLANCE

Movement Skill Objective Use the entire body to move expressively in stationary position

K–4 Dance Standard 1g Demonstrate kinesthetic awareness in performing movement skills

Physical Education Standard 1 Demonstrate competency in motor skills and movement patterns needed to perform a variety of physical activities

MATERIALS

* *Whirlwind*
  Teachers' Edition, Gr. 3, p. 149   **CD 5-19**

DANCE COUNT SEQUENCE

Count in sets of fast 8; 50 sets of 8 total

Section	Count
Introducion	4 sets of 8
Section 1	10 sets of 8
Section 2	8 sets of 8
Section 3	18 sets of 8
Section 4	10 sets of 8 + 4

1 Prepare

Warm Up

While students are seated, ask them to laugh out loud. Give visual **cues** to start and stop the laughing. Place your hands on your own shoulders. When you lift yours hands students can laugh. When your hands come back to your shoulders, students must stop laughing. Experiment with different types of laughing sounds.

SAY Make sure you are completely silent when you see the cue to stop laughing.

2 Take Action

Formation

Assign, or allow students to choose, places on the floor as their "laughing spots."

SAY Make sure you have plenty of room to move without touching anyone else. Stay in your own laughing spot.

Using the same visual cues as in the warm up, have students laugh silently.

SAY Make no sound.

Action

Cue the silent laughing.

Note: All movements for this activity are stationary.

SAY Perform any movement you want, but make sure that you watch my hands so that you can see the cue.

Watch for students who move in a fairly exaggerated manner and invite a few of them to demonstrate. Have the watchers **replay** the moves that are demonstrated. Name each demonstrated movement after its originator. Cue those movements by name, for example

SAY Everybody do the "Molly."

Then everyone should move the way "Molly" demonstrated.

Moving with Music

Play the recording of *Whirlwind* **CD 5-19** and ask students to laugh silently to the music. Help them to develop larger moves by involving various parts of the body. Experiment with "laugh dancing" while sitting, kneeling, lying on the back or stomach, standing, spinning, or jumping in place.

SAY Use more wiggly arm moves.

—Or—

SAY Try going down to the floor and getting back up again.

Play the music again and allow half of the class to share their laugh dances with the other half.

SAY As you watch, look for movement ideas that you would like to borrow for your own laugh dance.

Play the recording another time and have ever develop individual laugh dances. The music can be used simply as atmosphere or background, or it can be used to carry out particular movement objectives in specific sections, as defined in the Dance Count Sequence.

One option for a stationary laugh dance sequence follows.

* **Introduction**—Laugh dance giggles.
* **Section 1**—Laugh dance on their backs or stomachs.
* **Section 2**—Laugh dance while getting up and going back down.
* **Section 3**—Laugh dance with wiggly arms and legs, twisting and bending torso.
* **Section 4**—Laugh dance with moves as big and fast as possible.
* **When music ends**—Freeze.

SAY Make sure you use your entire body.

3 Reflect

Cool Down

String together three short laugh moves generated by three different students. Have the entire class perform them in unison and in slow motion.

SAY Move together by watching and sensing the rest of the class.

Have them end as laughing **statues**.

3 To Stand or Not to Stand

LESSON AT A GLANCE

Movement Skill Objective Maintain balance while changing the base of support at various levels

K–4 Dance Standard 1c Create shapes at low, middle, and high levels

Physical Education Standard 1 Demonstrate competency in movement patterns needed to perform a variety of physical activities

MATERIALS
- *Dances from Terpsichore,* "Bransle de la Torche" Teachers' Edition, Gr. 3, p. 63   **CD 2-39**

DANCE COUNT SEQUENCE
Count in sets of 8 at a moderate tempo.

Section	Music Cue	Count
Section A	Violin	4 sets of 8
Section B	Descending violin	4 sets of 8
Section C	Flute	4 sets of 8
Section D	Descending violin	4 sets of 8
Section E	Violin into flute	4 sets of 8
Section F	Violin into flute	8 sets of 8

1 Prepare

Warm Up
Have a discussion with students about the meaning of the term *base of support*.

SAY When you are standing, the feet are the base of support.

ASK What is your base of support right now?

2 Take Action

Formation
Students are seated in **grid** formation.

Positions and Moves
Play the recording of *Dances from Terpsichore,* "Bransle de la Torche" **CD 2-39** and instruct students to move with the music as follows.

- **Section A**—Begin in a seated **straddle** position. Students keep their legs straight and their backs flat; have them reach slowly and smoothly in various directions.

SAY Move carefully and stretch your muscles.

- **Section B**—Change the base of support to the hands and knees. Curve, arch, and twist the torso, keeping the base of support in the hands and knees.

SAY Stretch like a cat.

- **Section C**—Stand in neutral. Have students move their bodies at any speed, filling up as much space as they can, but never moving their feet.

SAY Feel free to bend your knees, but keep your feet flat on the floor. Expand yourself into the space in all directions.

- **Section D**—Have students use one foot or the other as the base of support. Move the **working leg** and concentrate on making unusual shapes with that leg, the arms, and torso, while one foot remains on the floor. Have the students tilt their bodies while they move the working leg.

ASK What can you do to help yourself keep your balance? (Concentrate weight on the base of support.)

- **Section E**—Have students lie face down and move slowly. Keeping the abdomen as the base of support, have students explore as much motion as they can.

SAY Keep the movements slow. Use all of your muscles, especially your back and abdomen.

- **Section F**—Have students roll onto their backs. Move at any tempo, keeping the spine as the base of support.

ASK What unique moves can you do with this base of support? (Encourage students to describe their movements.)

3 Reflect

Cool Down
As a group, create amusing base of support combinations such as two hands and one foot, one foot and one hand, or two hands and two feet. Have students observe how many solutions they can come up with for each different base of support.

4 Stop and Go

LESSON AT A GLANCE

Movement Skill Objective Demonstrate the ability to move and rest in quick reaction on command

K–4 Dance Standard 1b Accurately demonstrate basic locomotor movements (such as walk, gallop, and skip)

Physical Education Standard 5 Exhibit responsible personal and social behavior that respects self and others in physical activity settings

MATERIALS

- "Can You Canoe?" Teachers' Edition, Gr. 4, p. 170 **CD 7-29**
- Drum and mallet

RECORDING ROUTINE

Intro (water sounds, then 4 m.); vocal 1 (16 m.); interlude (4 m.); vocal 2 (16 m.); interlude (4 m.); vocal 3 (16 m.); coda (free)

DANCE NOTE

The music is in compound meter and gets progressively faster with each repetition.

1 Prepare

Warm Up

Have students walk around the room at their own pace. Then have them **skip** or **gallop** when you give a verbal **cue**. Observe whether they understand the difference between the two movements. (See Movement Glossary for definitions.)

2 Take Action

Formation

Permit students to move around the room freely to experience the distinctly different sensations of walking, skipping, and galloping rhythms.

SAY Respect the space of your classmates as you move.

Practice Moving

Have students **walk** to the beat or rhythms you play on a drum. The rhythms shown above right can signal whether students should walk, skip, or gallop. Demonstrate and name the rhythms. Note that the notated rhythm for skip is the same as the rhythm for gallop except that the skip starts on an upbeat.

For the skipping rhythm play the upbeat on the rim of the drum (indicated with the "x" noteheads) to help students aurally distinguish it from the galloping rhythm.

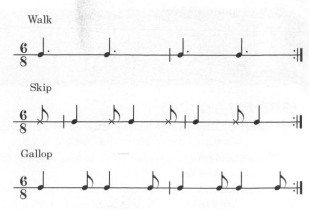

Instruct students to listen for the rhythm cues to walk, skip, or gallop. You may need to add verbal cues for skipping and galloping until they hear the distinction between the two.

Stop and Go with the Music

Play the recording of "Can You Canoe?" **CD 7-29.** Have students listen one time through, patting the beat on their thighs. Make sure they notice and attend to the tempo changes with each repetition. Play the recording again. Have them move as follows in response to the music.

- **Introduction**—Stand still and snap or bop on the offbeats (4 measures or 8 counts).
- **Vocal 1**—Skip around the room in time with the music (16 measures or 4 sets of 8 counts).
- **Interlude**—Stop, stand still, and snap or bop on the offbeats while music gets faster (4 measures or 8 counts).
- **Vocal 2**—Gallop around the room in time with the music (16 measures or 4 sets of 8 counts).
- **Interlude**—Stop, stand still, and snap or bop on the offbeats while music gets faster (4 measures or 8 counts).
- **Vocal 3**—Walk around the room, stepping energetically on the beat (16 measures or 4 sets of 8 counts).
- **Coda**—Stop and listen, remain stationar perform movements in response to the music and then the water sounds.

3 Reflect

Cool Down

Repeat the warm up activity. Then have students sit and clap the walking rhythm, snap-clap the skipping rhythm, and pat (right-left) the galloping rhythm.

5 Put the Beat in the Body

LESSON AT A GLANCE

Movement Skill Objective Isolate rhythm patterns and demonstrate them in movement

K–4 Dance Standard 1f Demonstrate accuracy in moving to a musical beat

Physical Education Standard 2 Demonstrate understanding of movement concepts, principles, and strategies as they apply to the performance of physical activities

MATERIALS

- *Thunder and Lightening Polka*
  Teachers' Edition, Gr. 4, p. 213   **CD 9-5**

DANCE COUNT SEQUENCE

Count in simple fast eights, except where other counts are indicated.

Section	Music Cue	Count
Intro		1 set of 8
Section A1	Drum flourishes	4 sets of 8 then 4 sets of 8 + 4 + 10
Section B1	Fast beat with cymbals	4 sets of 8 then 4 sets of 8 then 1 set of 8
Section C	Clarinet smooth melody	4 sets of 8 then 4 sets of 8
Section D	Chirping violins	4 sets of 8 then 4 sets of 8 + 6
Section E	Violins with cymbals	4 sets of 8
Section A2	Drum flourishes	4 sets of 8 then 4 sets of 8 + 4 + 10
Section B2	Fast beat with cymbals	4 sets of 8 then 4 sets of 8
Coda	Big chords	8 + 6 + 4 + 8 + 3

1 Prepare

Warm Up

Have students stand and **mirror** each other in slow motion, but with no assigned leader. Each partnership must work as a team and create moves using the entire body.

SAY Keep your eyes on each other at all times, avoid moves that turn away from your partner.

2 Take Action

Formation

Have students work with partners. Carefully organize the positioning of the **partnerships** around the room so that each pair has plenty of space to work for this stationary activity. Have one partner face the other so that both partners are in profile to **downstage** (the front of the room).

Each partnership should invent a **movement cue** or signal that switches the lead from one partner to the other. Each partnership will have its own unique cue. Students can sit, stand, or lie on their backs, sides, or stomachs, as long as they can see each other's eyes.

SAY Make sure to share the lead with your partner.

Move to the Music

Play the recording of *Thunder and Lightening Polka* **CD 9-5**. Beginning with one leader in each partnership, have students move in a very rhythmic, choppy fashion. Have them **isolate** the rhythm in one or two parts of the body at a time.

SAY Use the beat in the music to help you move.

Partnerships switch the lead by using their own invented cue. Suggest that they use the different sections of the music as places to change movement patterns. Encourage students to repeat their moves a number of times before trying a new move.

SAY Make a **movement pattern** as you experiment with the beat.

Students should use as many parts of the body as they can to invent isolated, rhythmic moves for their partners to mirror. Ask students to use changes in level or shape in addition to the rhythmic isolations they are making.

After the music ends, ask the partnerships to continue leading and switching two more times in silence.

SAY Move to the same beat you heard when the music was playing.

3 Reflect

Cool Down

With the class seated, ask each student to say his or her name three ways. Have the class echo each version. The first version should be *staccato* (or short and separated), the second *legato* (or smooth and connected), and the third should have many extra beats or syllables in it.

SAY Experiment with making rhythms with your name and demonstrate them in movement.

LESSON 3 — To Stand or Not to Stand

LESSON AT A GLANCE

Movement Skill Objective   Change levels and the base of support in a movement sequence

5–8 Dance Standard 1a   Demonstrate the following movement skills and explain the underlying principles: alignment, balance, initiation of movement, and weight shift

Physical Education Standard 1   Demonstrate competency in movement patterns

MATERIALS
- *Wipe Out*
  Teachers' Edition, Gr. 5, p. 155   **CD 8-3**

DANCE NOTE
Count in sets of eight beats during the music.

1 Prepare

Warm Up

With students in **home spots,** verbally direct them to change their bases of support several times.

SAY Two feet, one hand, one foot, abdomen, two hands, one foot (and so on).

2 Take Action

Formation

Home spots.

Create the Movement Sequence

Play the recording of *Wipe Out* **CD 8-3.** Have students use the music as background and remain stationary as they create and memorize a sequence of eight positions that use different bases of support. Encourage them to change levels often.

SAY Think of unusual ways to support yourself. You must be able to hold the position and not fall out of it.

Once each student has his or her own sequence memorized, have all students change their positions on count one and hold for counts two through eight.

SAY Find the balance in your base of support.

Next, move through the sequence twice as fast, switching positions on count one and holding for counts two through four and then change.

SAY Think ahead. Do not let your next move surprise you.

3 Reflect

Discussion

Lead a discussion about commonly used bases of support.

SAY Name some activities that regularly use unusual bases of support.

LESSON 4 — Stop and Go

LESSON AT A GLANCE

Movement Skill Objective   Create and perform basic loco-motor step sequences, including walking, skipping, jogging, and hopping, in follow-the-leader fashion

5–8 Dance Standard 1b   Students accurately identify and demonstrate basic dance steps and patterns for dance

Physical Education Standard 2   Demonstrate understanding of movement principles and tactics as they apply to the learning and performance of physical activities

MATERIALS
- *Take Five (excerpt)*
  Teachers' Edition, Gr. 5, p. 220   **CD 10-37**

DANCE COUNT SEQUENCE
Count in quick sets of five.

Section	Music Cue	Count
Intro	Cymbal	4 sets of 5
Section A	Piano enters	4 sets of 5 then 4 sets of 5
Section B1	Saxophone enters	4 sets of 5 then 4 sets of 5
Section C	Sax gets higher	4 sets of 5 then 4 sets of 5
Section B2	Saxophone as in B1	4 sets of 5 then 4 sets of 5

DANCE NOTE
Set the CD player to auto repeat for this track.

1 Prepare

Warm Up

Have students work in **partnerships** in a game of follow-the-leader, using simple **locomotor** movements. With the entire class working at the same time, have students create various traveling steps or patterns. Allow them to choose when to switch from leading to following.

SAY Stay close to your partner and concentrate on interesting ways to move your feet. Keep locomoting. Be aware of the other partnerships in the space. No bumping, please.

2 Take Action

Formation

Arrange groups of five students in follow-the-leader type lines. Movements should always travel for or sideward without any turns. Leaders must demonstrate consistent steps that the followers can easily imitate.

Move to Five

Play the music *Take Five* **CD 10-37** five times through. Have each student in the group **lead** a set of locomotor movements around the room. The entire class should work at the same time, with each unique line being sensitive to sharing the space.

SAY Keep your own line intact. Do not cut through any other lines and keep plenty of space around you.

Ask each leader to vary the steps when they hear the music sections change. Each leader should be able to travel in at least two distinct steps or patterns.

SAY Leaders, your goal is to make sure your team is moving in **unison**.

Simple moves such as quick walking, skipping, or jogging are fine, or leaders may wish to create more complicated traveling steps.

SAY Try galloping, sliding, or performing **grapevine** steps. Try hopping or high-stepping kicks. Remember, no turns or going backwards.

When the music stops to reset the track, have the line leaders move to the end of the line, giving high-fives to the rest of the group as they pass. Now the second person in line is the new leader.

SAY Leaders, remember to give your team something they can follow. Do not change your pattern too soon.

After the fifth sequence of repeats, the first leader will be back in front. Stop the recording. In silence and stationary, have students high-five each other, one after the other down the line. After the last high five, have the entire class say *five* in a whispered voice. Ask the class to work out a visual **cue** so that the word can be delivered together.

3 Reflect

Cool Down

Working as one ensemble, have students slowly, silently, and continuously walk around the space. When eye contact is made with one other person, travel along with that person until something breaks the eye contact. Students may be close to or quite spread apart in relation to their eye contact partners. Eye contact partners may change often and randomly, depending on the students' **pathways.**

SAY Concentrate on keeping your eye-to-eye connection going until there is a natural break in the connection.

---

5 Put the Beat in the Body

LESSON AT A GLANCE

Movement Skill Objective   Perform beat and rhythm through locomotor movements

5–8 Dance Standard 1d   Accurately transfer a rhythmic pattern from the aural to the kinesthetic

Physical Education Standard 2   Demonstrate understanding of movement principles as they apply to the performance of physical activities

MATERIALS
- "Ama-Lama" Teachers' Edition, Gr. 5, p. 142   **CD 7-15**
- Drum with mallet

RECORDING ROUTINE

Intro (4 m.); vocal A (4 m.); vocal B (4 m.); vocal A (4 m.); vocal C (4 m.); vocal A (4 m.); vocal A (4 m.); vocal B (4 m.); vocal A (4 m.); vocal C (4 m.); vocal A (4 m.); coda

1 Prepare

Warm Up

Play a steady rhythm on the drum and have students walk to the beat. On your signal, have students **gallop.** On a different signal have them pat the beats.

2 Take Action

Organize the class into three groups—A, B, and C. Have students stand shoulder to shoulder in two to four lines per group.

Moving to the Beat

Call out the group letters and have the groups perform these movements.

- **Group A**—Gallop forward 6 beats and clap 2 beats. Gallop backward (to place) 6 beats and clap 2 beats.

- **Group B**—Walk forward 6 beats and clap 2 beats. Walk backward 6 beats and clap 2 beats.

- **Group C**—Slide to right side 6 beats and clap 2 beats. Slide to left side 6 beats and clap 2 beats.

Play the recording of "Ama-Lama" **CD 7-15** and have groups move in the same sequence as the song. Help them by cueing the group letters (see Recording Routine).

3 Reflect

Cool Down

While students are seated, ask them to put their groups' movements into their hands. Call out the letter names of the groups and have students mime their group's patterns.

6 The Balanced Body

LESSON AT A GLANCE

Movement Skill Objective   Perform sequences that combine balancing and weight transfer

5–8 Dance Standard 1a   Demonstrate balance and weight transfer

Physical Education Standard 1   Demonstrate competency in motor skills needed to perform a variety of physical activities

MATERIALS

- *The Moon Mirrored in the Pool* Teachers' Edition, Gr. 6, p. 103   **CD 6-19**

DANCE SEQUENCE

Section	Music Cue	Movement Cue
Intro [to :06]	Short flute solo	Floor shape
Section A [:06–:31]	Full ensemble sound	Right foot balance
Section B [:31–1:16]	Rhythmic with string solo	Left foot balance
Section C [1:16–2:20]	Solo string over tremolos	Rotate on one foot
Section D [2:20–end]	Full ensemble sound	Tilt

1 Prepare

Warm Up

Have students spread out in the space, facing any direction. After standing quietly in neutral with eyes closed for a few moments, have students open their eyes and fix them on an immoveable object at eye level. Keeping focused on that object, have them imagine that their muscles have turned into steel. Then each student should slowly lift one leg and balance. Experiment with slowly moving various parts of the body while maintaining a simple balance on a flat foot. Repeat on the other side.

2 Take Action

Formation

Students spread out generously in the space. In stationary position, have each student melt to the floor into a beginning shape.

Movement Sequence

Play the recording of *The Moon Mirrored in the Pool* **CD 6-19**. The movement sequence begins after the short introduction.

- **Section A**—Slowly grow up into a standing balance on the right foot. Gently allow the arms to move as if they are floating in a slight breeze.

SAY Focus your eyes on something that will not move.

- **Section B**—Melt back down to the floor and rewind the motions back up on the left foot. Float the arms again while balancing on this side.

SAY Make your muscles feel very tight, but make your limbs look like silk moving in the wind.

- **Section C**—Find balance on the right foot with arms held still in an outstretched, **asymmetrical** position. Gently rotate at the waist **clockwise**, maintaining the balance on the right foot with arms held in position. **Reverse** the direction and balance on the left foot, rotating **counterclockwise**.

SAY As you rotate, move your **standing foot** bits, as if your foot is the second hand of a clock.

- **Section D**—Balance on one foot and then the other, slowly moving the **working leg** head or torso. Always maintain balance as the body shifts through various off-centered positions.

SAY See how much space you can fill with your body and still keep your balance.

3 Reflect

Cool Down

Remaining stationary and moving in slow motion, have students move through a variety of positions with their eyes closed. Positions can progress through balancing, changing levels, and rotating, but movement must remain slow and controlled.

7 Airborne Action

LESSON AT A GLANCE

Movement Skill Objective Perform airborne movements with smooth landings

5–8 Dance Standard 1a Demonstrate movement skills with elevation and landing

Physical Education Standard 2 Apply involvement concepts and principals to the learning and development of motor skills

MATERIALS
* *Black Suits Comin' (Nod Ya Head)*
  Teachers' Edition, Gr. 7, p. A-5   **CD 1-6**

DANCE COUNT SEQUENCE
Count in moderate eights.

Section	Music Cue	Count
Intro	Distortion guitar	2 sets of 8
Section A	Trumpets enter, rapping	5 sets of 8
Section B	*I guarantee*	4 sets of 8
Section C	*Black suits*	4 sets of 8
Section D1	*Nod ya head*	4 sets of 8
Section E	*There's this*	4 sets of 8
Section F	Strings enter, rapping	4 sets of 8
Section D2	*Nod ya head*	4 sets of 8

1 Prepare

Background
Share with the class that the music used in this lesson was featured in the box office hit movie *Men in Black II*.

Warm Up
In order to help students warm up and stretch out their leg muscles, perform a number of basic leg exercises. First, have them stand in neutral and slowly roll the head down to the floor, keeping the knees straight. Hang for a moment and recover back up to neutral. Next, with feet together and parallel, slowly bend and straighten the knees, keeping the feet flat on the floor. Finally, have students stand in an easy first position. Do eight *grande pliés* in **first position** as follows.

* Slowly move into a squat position with toes turned outward, spine straight up and down.

* Recover by slowly coming back up.

SAY Use and stretch your leg muscles at the same time. If a muscle feels like it is pulling, relax it or bend your knees just a little.

2 Take Action

Formation
Organize the class into three to five groups of students. Groups travel through **space columns** without overlapping the next column. Depending on the shape and size of the classroom, set these space columns vertically or horizontally. Assign a group for each column and have the group members line up behind each other at the head of each column. Use as many space columns as will fit into the room comfortably.

Airborne Sequence
Play the recording of *Black Suits Comin' (Nod Ya Head)* **CD 1-6** and use the music as a background beat; it is not necessary to coordinate with any particular section. Instruct students to travel through the space quickly, using a step that naturally involves elevation, such as **skipping, galloping,** or slow **jogging.** Have students stylize their bodies and attitudes to match the feel of the music. Have each student go through his or her own columns and back, one after the other. One student from each column can move at the same time.

SAY Use the beat in the music to make your moves. Get yourself airborne.

As the music continues, have students travel through the column again, one student per column. This time, run into the column and do one very high **leap,** taking off on one foot and landing on the other, making a **held shape** with the upper body. The shape should be reminiscent of the characters in *Men in Black II*.

ASK How high can you leap? How far can you go?

For the last pass through the space columns, have students travel by jumping, **hopping,** or leaping without many **connecting steps** between the airborne moves. The motion should go continually forward. Connect the movements with the rhythm of the music and the attitude of the lyrics.

SAY Concentrate on making a smooth landing. Make no noise when you land. Stay in the air as long as you can.

3 Reflect

Discussion
Lead a discussion with students about how the feet, ankles, and knees work together to achieve height in a jump and a smooth landing. Ask them to consider the way springs, trampolines, and other shock absorbing systems work.

9 Moving to the Glossary

LESSON AT A GLANCE

Movement Skill Objective   Perform folk dance steps and modern dance steps in a sequence and move as a unified ensemble

5–8 Dance Standard 1h   Describe the action and movement elements observed in a dance, using appropriate movement/dance vocabulary

Physical Education Standard 6   Demonstrate understanding and respect for differences among people in physical activity settings

MATERIALS
- *Flight of the Ibis*
  Teachers' Edition, Gr. 8, p. D-16   **CD 8-21**
- *Two Dances for Three Xylophones* "Hornpipe and Jig"
  Teachers' Edition, Gr. 8, p. D-17   **CD 8-22**

DANCE COUNT SEQUENCE

Count in moderate sets of eights.
Begin with **CD 8-21.**

Section	Movement Cue	Count
Section A	Step touch into circle	4 sets of 8
Section B	Sashay	4 sets of 8
Section C	Fast pathway and buzz step	4 sets of 8
Section D	Line and grapevine, body percussion	4 sets of 8
Section E	Gallop pathway and collapse	4 sets of 8
Section F	Partner allemandes	4 sets of 8
Section G	Invented pattern pathway	4 sets of 8
Section H	Grid 360° and circle pathway	2 sets of 8 + 4

Play through into **CD 8-22** until **0:41** only.

Section	Movement Cue	Count
Section A	Circle step touch	2 sets of 8
Section B	Sashay	2 sets of 8
Section C	Fast pathway and buzz step	2 sets of 8
Section D	Line and grapevine body percussion	2 sets of 8
Section E	Gallop pathway and collapse	2 sets of 8

DANCE NOTE

This lesson builds skills in movement memory, thinking and dancing at the same time, and performing steps in unison. The moves used for the lesson combine the contrasting styles of folk dance and modern dance.

1 Prepare

Warm Up

Invite students to warm up their memory skills with the short game *I'm Going to California*. In cir 4–6 students, one student says "I'm going to California and I'm bringing a—." The next student says "I'm going to California and I'm bringing [whatever the first student brought] and a—." The third says "I'm going to California and I'm bringing [whatever the first and second students brought] and a—." Continue around the circle.

2 Take Action

Formations

With students seated in the space, tell them that they will be creating four group formations—a circle, a horizontal line, a partnership, and a grid. Using the four words *circle, line, partnership, grid* as **cues**, have students move as an entire group as quickly as possible, without touching or talking, into each formation. Do this activity in silence except for your verbal cues. Stay upbeat as you give the instructions.

SAY You have ten counts from the time I call the cue for the entire class to get into the right formation. No touching, no talking. *Circle*—ten, nine, eight, seven, six, five, four, three, two, one.

Cueing the Formations

Call out the cues *circle, line, partnership,* and few times each. Vary the order in which you call the cues and the length of time you allow for students to arrive at each formation. The students should remember exactly who they are standing next to, exactly where the formation is in space, and exactly which direction they are facing. In other words, they should reproduce the formations the same way every time the cue is called.

SAY Go to the exact same place every time. Remember who your neighbors are in each formation.

As students arrive in each formation, have them face a specific direction for each formation. *Circle* inside, *line* faces **down stage**, *partnership* faces a partner, and *grid* faces down stage.

Continuing to build within these formations, drill each group as it arrives at the formation as follows.

- **Circle**—Students jog **clockwise (CW)** or **counterclockwise (CCW)**, keeping the spaces even.

- **Line**—Students jump and face the **stage direction** you ask them to face, for example,

SAY Up stage (point your finger away from the audience), down stage (point your finger toward the audience), **stage right** (point your finger to the right of the stage), **stage left** (point your finger to the left of the stage).

- **Partnerships**—Partners stay about arm's length away from each other and shake right hands, then left hands.
- **Grid**—Students should form a grid of four to eight across and as many lines deep as needed to accommodate the class size and space in which the activity is taking place.

SAY Find a window in the line, or lines, in front of you. Stay in your own spot.

The Steps

Play the recordings of *Flight of the Ibis* **CD 8-21** and *Two Dances for Three Xylophones* "Hornpipe and Jig" **CD 8-22** to keep an underlying beat, then teach the following steps to the class while they are in grid formation. Explain that after they learn these steps, they will combine them with the formations and pathways to complete the dance sequence.

- **Three Steps and a Touch**—Walk forward right-left-right and then **touch** (or tap) with left (R-L-R-L touch). Repeat on alternate side, but go backwards beginning on left (L-R-L-R touch).
- **Sashay**—Side step smoothly, side-close, side-close, and so on. Do three to the right and pause, then three to the left and pause.
- **Buzz Step**—Keeping one foot in place and using the ball of the foot of the other, **pivot** around the foot. The movement can go clockwise and counterclockwise on each foot.

SAY Make sure that you stay in the same spot while you pivot.

- **Grapevine**—Step side-back-side-front. Practice the grapevine to a very slow steady beat and then practice it double time, or twice as fast.

SAY Keep your knees slightly bent for the entire step. Do not twist your shoulders.

- **Gallop**—This basic step does not alternate sides. The front foot goes higher and back foot catches up, repeating on the same side.
- **Allemande Left and Right**—Facing partners, take left hands and walk around each other counterclockwise in 8 counts. Switch to right hands and walk around each other clockwise.

Pathways

In order to develop spatial memory, have students walk slowly for 8 counts in one direction, then pause, turn around, and rewind the pattern exactly. Pause, turn around again, and repeat several times.

SAY Use your eyes, ears, and **muscle memory** to recreate your pathway.

The Glossary Dance Sequence

Play the recording again, starting with **CD 8-21**. The following instructions clarify how to perform each dance cue. After students learn the steps in sequence, use the Dance Count Sequence in the Lesson-at-a-Glance to give the cues.

- **Section A**—In circle, step-touch in and out of circle 4 times.

- **Section B**—In circle, sashay 8 counts counterclockwise, then 8 counts clockwise. Repeat.
- **Section C**—Travel on individual pathways for 8 counts. Buzz step 8 counts. For second 8-count pathway, end up in a group horizontal line. Buzz step counterclockwise in line, using left foot as the pivot.
- **Section D**—Perform alternating 4-count grapevines. Go right first. Add improvised body percussion on the last 2 sets of 8.
- **Section E**—Gallop on individual pathways for 8 counts. Collapse to the floor and recover into standing neutral for 8 counts. Repeat, but use pathways to get into partner positions and perform second collapse there.
- **Section F**—Alternate left and right allemandes, 8 counts in each direction.
- **Section G**—Taking four sets of 8 to arrive at their grid spots, students invent an individual 4-count pattern and repeat it on their own pathway.
- **Section H**—Taking 2 counts per direction, jump from both feet to both feet in quarter circles. First go clockwise, then counterclockwise. For the last 8, perform two 360° turns in place, 4 counts each. Adjust into circle, then silence.

Continue by playing CD 8-22 (stop at the end of the "Hornpipe" at 0:41).

Use the same sequence of steps up through Section E with this different music and perform the sequence as shown in the Dance Count Sequence in the Lesson-at-a-Glance.

SAY Concentrate on counting and moving your feet quickly and cleanly. This section ends when you collapse. Make it a good one.

3 Reflect

Cool Down

Seated with their eyes closed, have students visualize the entire movement sequence from this lesson. Have them replay the sequence in their minds two times. With their eyes open and remaining seated, have students dance the sequence using only their hands and arms. Have students describe what they have performed.

ASK Using your hands like puppets, how many details can you put in with your hands?

SAY Remember the formations, pathways, steps, rhythm, and sequence.

Patterned Movement

What Is Patterned Movement?

Patterned movement is one of the general terms used to describe movement activities such as folk dances, social dances, riser choreographies, classroom arrangements of ethnic and popular dances, and singing games.

Patterned movement and dance use the same concepts and skills that creative, improvised, and freeform dance and movement use. A characteristic that distinguishes patterned movement and dance from the other movement forms is the presence of a predictable structure that uses particular formations, specific steps, and repeated phrases. The dance steps fit the musical phrases and usually have a specific styling.

Folk dances have historical and cultural backgrounds and are usually handed down through generations. The dances that are currently performed are the same or similar to the original dances.

Patterned, creative, improvised, and choreographed dances often cross over into one another's territories. A classroom folk dance may have originally come from the creative effort of an individual or group; many international recreational dances were adapted from choreographies of ethnic ensembles. Over the years, these creative efforts and choreographies became fixed enough to be transmitted in the same or in similar forms, finally evolving into patterned dances.

Traditional dances of a culture combine several types. They have particular formations, repeated rhythms, regular phrasing, and specific styling. In addition to the basic structure, traditional dances usually include some form of improvisation and opportunities for creativity. Examples of this type of traditional dance include the Arabic *debky,* the Argentinean *tango,* the Greek *hasapikos,* and swing dancing of the United States.

Riser choreography can enhance singing performances on stage and in the classroom. It uses basic formations, visual effects, and simple gestures that help to add energy and meaning for the performers and the audience.

The patterned dances in this Sampler Book have been chosen because they offer a variety of movement skills, formations, cultures, classroom usefulness, and historical contexts, including dances from specific time periods in the United States.

2 A Getting-Started Activity

LESSON AT A GLANCE

Movement Skill Objective   Successfully perform nonlocomotor and locomotor activities in time with music

K–4 Dance Standard 1g   Students show kinesthetic awareness, concentration, and focus in performing movement skills

Physical Education Standard 2   Demonstrate understanding of movement concepts as they apply to the learning of physical activities

MATERIALS
• "Mashed Potatoes"
  Teachers' Edition, Gr. 1, p. 20
• Mixing bowls, spoons, toy cooking utensils

RECORDING ROUTINE
Intro (8 m.); spoken verse (16 m.); sung refrain (6 m.); interlude (16 m.); spoken verse and sung refrain (22 m.), coda

DANCE NOTE
After doing the teacher-led pattern, you may wish to encourage the children to insert their own ideas.

1 Prepare

Background
Share with the children that "Mashed Potatoes" is a call-and response song from the French-speaking, Creole culture of Louisiana, called Zydeco.

Note: The music is percussive, syncopated, and humorous.

Warm Up
Ask children to move as if preparing food, using the lyrics of the song for ideas. Choose appropriate movements to incorporate into the activity

2 Take Action

Formation
Students sit on the floor in several rows in front of the teacher. Play the recording of "Mashed Potatoes" **CD 1-32** and have the children per actions for each of the musical sections as follows.

Introduction
Children lightly pat legs, alternating hands, and quietly pulse their bodies to the beat.

Spoken Verse
In call-and–response fashion, demonstrate the movements that were chosen during the W activity. Have the children respond by repeating them after you.

SAY Be sure to keep the beat of the song.

Sung Refrain

- With one arm rounded in front (holding bowl), stir four times with a (pretend) spoon.
- Scoop and eat potatoes four times.
- Rub tummy in appreciation three times.

Instrumental Interlude

- Stand and walk 16 steps in scattered formation, hands clasped behind back, as if waiting for potatoes to be ready.
- Look at wristwatch (4 beats), make a heavy sigh (4 beats), then sit again in original spot to be ready for repeat of song (8 beats).

Repeat movements for verse and refrain.

Coda

Rub tummies for 6 counts, then say "Yum!"

Review

Play the song recording again and have the children perform the sequence of actions. Observe whether they perform the appropriate movements in time with the music.

3 Reflect

Discussion

Discuss with the children whether they felt they were able to keep the beat as they moved with the music.

Cool Down

Invite the children to suggest other foods to prepare and demonstrate appropriate gestures for them. Use the Stereo Performance **CD 1-33** as accompaniment.

Have the children "call" the movements and you "respond" by repeating them, or have half of the class "call" and the other half respond.

———————————

6 Circle Dance from French Canada

LESSON AT A GLANCE

Movement Skill Objective Move in a circle, change direction, and hold the *fermata*

K–4 Dance Standard 1f Demonstrate accuracy in moving to a beat and responding to changes in tempo

Physical Education Standard 1 Demonstrate competency in movement patterns

MATERIALS

- *Les saluts*
  Teachers' Edition, Gr. 1, p. 363   **CD 11-25, 26**

DANCE COUNT SEQUENCE

Intro (4 beats); A1 (CW 16 counts); A2 (CCW 16 counts); B (4 + 4 + 4 + *fermata* + 4 counts); repeat from A1 through B; repeat again from A1 at slower tempo with gradual *accelerando* to B

1 Prepare

Warm Up

Play the Dance Practice Tempo recording of *Les saluts* **CD 11-26** and have the children walk to the beat. Help them to recognize the *fermata* and show them how to bow and hold.

2 Take Action

Children stand in a single circle with hands in **V hold**.

The Steps

A1—All walk to the left or **clockwise (CW)** for 16 counts.

A2—All walk to the right or **counterclockwise (CCW)** for 16 counts.

B—Move as follows

- All walk forward to the center for 4 counts.
- Walk backward out of the center for 4 counts.
- Walk into the center again for 4 counts.
- Bow during the *fermata* (about 4 counts)
- Move backward to place for the last 4 counts.

Play the Dance Practice recording for the whole pattern. When the children are able to competently change directions on the phrases and hold the bow, play the Dance Performance recording **CD 11-25** and have them perform the dance all the way through.

3 Reflect

Discussion

ASK What was the hardest part of this dance? How did the music change at the end? (Allow the children to share their experiences and ideas.)

LESSON
8 Texas Play Party

LESSON AT A GLANCE

Movement Skill Objective   Use the V hold, skater's hand hold, and elbow turns while participating in a social dance with partners and corners

K–4 Dance Standard 5a   Perform folk dances from various cultures with competence and confidence

Physical Education Standards 1   Demonstrate competency in motor skills and movement patterns needed to perform a variety of physical activities

MATERIALS
• "Shake Them 'Simmons Down"
   Teachers' Edition, Gr. 2, p. 244   **CD 8-34**
• Persimmons or pictures of persimmons

RECORDING ROUTINE
Intro (8 m.); verses 1–6 (8 mm. each); interlude (8 m.); verses 1–6

DANCE NOTE
This song assumes boys and girls are partners, as is true in most traditional dances. If, however, the dance would be more successful as nongender specific, use ones and twos, or reds and blues, or ties and kerchiefs, or other creative labels.

As a language tie-in, the class might discuss the grammar of shaking *them 'simmons*.

1 Prepare

Background
This Texas play party sings about shaking the persimmon tree to make the fruit fall.

Warm Up
Have children sit in a circle next to partners to learn the song. Play the Dance Performance recording of "Shake Them 'Simmons Down" **CD 8-34** and have the children lean right, left, center, and so on, following the words of the song. Have the children practice, using the **skater's hand hold.**

SKATER'S HAND HOLD

2 Take Action

Formation
All stand in a circle with hands joined in the In each pair *ones* (boys) are on the left of *twos* (girls). Make sure the children know who are their partners and corners are. Play the recording and have children perform the following actions.

• **Verse 1** *Circle right, . . .*
   All walk **counterclockwise (CCW)** 16 steps.

• **Verse 2** *Circle left, . . .*
   All walk **clockwise (CW)** 16 steps.

• **Verse 3** *Boys to the center, . . .*
   Ones walk to the center 4 steps and back out 4 steps, while *twos* clap on the beat. Repeat.

• **Verse 4** *Girls to the center, . . .*
   Twos walk to the center 4 steps and back out 4 steps, while *ones* clap on the beat. Repeat.

SAY As *twos* back out, take the skater's position and turn to walk counterclockwise. *Twos* are on the outside, *ones* are on the inside.

• **Verse 5** *Promenade all, . . .*
   In skater's position, partners walk 12 steps CCW.

On the next 4 counts—

SAY Drop your partner's hands and hook right elbows with your corners.

• **Verse 6** *Swing your corner, . . .*
   With corners, do a right **elbow turn** for 8 counts, then a left elbow turn for 8 counts.

SAY As you unhook elbows, stay beside your corner—your new partner!—and join hands to circle right again. Twos are on the right.

Review
Invite the children to perform the dance all the way through with the recording. Observe their ability to perform the sequence of movements, using the V hold, skater's position, and elbow turns competently and smoothly.

3 Reflect

Discussion
ASK Were you able to go smoothly from the skater's hand hold with your partners to the elbow turn with your corners? (Allow for an open discussion on ways to improve the performance or for sharing about their enjoyment of the dance.)

9 Ev'ry Kind of Movement

LESSON AT A GLANCE

Movement Skill Objective Perform a stationary movement sequence while singing a song

K–4 Dance Standard 1f Demonstrate accuracy in moving to a musical beat and responding to changes in tempo

Physical Education Standard 2 Demonstrate understanding of movement concepts and strategies as they apply to the performance of physical activities

MATERIALS

- "Ev'ry Kind of Music"
Teachers' Edition, Gr. 2, p. 226   **CD 8-14**

RECORDING ROUTINE

Intro (free organ, 3 m.); vocal (16 m.); instrumental (16 m.); vocal (16 m.);

MOVEMENT SEQUENCE

Section	Lyric Cue	Movement Cue
Introduction 1		Organ waves
Introduction 2		Funky drums
Section 1	*Ev'ry kind of music,*	Hands to knees
Section 2	*Gotta have music,*	Hands to hips
Section 3	*Give me lots of music*	Hands to knees
Section 4	*to sing and dance and play.*	Finger bops/ hand flash
Section 5	*Feel the beat a movin',*	Hands to knees
Section 6	*Singin' a song to make my day,*	Finger bop
Section 7	*Makes me swing and sway*	Slow sways
Section 8	*Singin' on the way.*	Fast sways
Dance Bridge 1		Violin
Dance Bridge 2		Saxophone
Dance Bridge 3		Asian dance
Dance Bridge 4		Float hands
Dance Bridge 5		Head bop & drums
Repeat song		
Coda		Bagpipes

1 Prepare

Warm Up

Seated on the floor, have children act out playing various orchestral instruments. **Cue** the group to start, stop, and change the tempo.

SAY Make it look like the instrument is really in your hands. Keep your eyes on the conductor.

2 Take Action

Formation

Children stand in a grid in **windows** (staggered so that all children can be seen) or on risers.

Stationary Choreography

See Movement Sequence for lyric and movement cues.

- **Introduction 1**—Move arms and body side to side with a spooky feeling, feet planted, each child improvising his or her own gestures.

Note: Work in unison from here on.

- **Introduction 2**—Move **in place** after the drum riff. Start with the right foot and alternate right and left: step-touch three measures, on the fourth measure, plant both feet.
- **Section 1**—Lean over, bounce hands on knees.
- **Section 2**—Stand straight up, hands on hips, head shaking up and down.
- **Section 3**—Lean over, bounce hands on knees, as in Section 1.
- **Section 4**—Perform four fast double finger-bops on *sing and dance and, on play* open palms and shake hands.
- **Section 5**—Lean over, bounce hands on knees, as in Section 1, continue through the word *singin'*.
- **Section 6**—Stand up and do five finger-bops on the words *song to make my day*.
- **Section 7**—Sway four beats, alternating R and L. Continue though *way*.
- **Section 8**—After cutoff, do three fast sways R-L-R, following the pulse of the music.

Dance Bridge note: The movements in the dance bridge happen in quick succession, changing precisely when the musical style changes. Use the sound of the instrumentation to cue the dance changes. Keep feet planted at all times.

- **Dance Bridge 1**—Act out playing the violin.
- **Dance Bridge 2**—Act out playing saxophone.
- **Dance Bridge 3**—Asian dance: hands above head, palms together flat, fingers pointing to ceiling, head wiggling.
- **Dance Bridge 4**—Float hands down, playing piano as they lower.
- **Dance Bridge 5**—Head and neck bop forward and back, and act out playing drums.

Repeat song exactly as above.

- **Coda**—Act out playing bagpipes. Pulse the elbows down and blow six times. At the start of the seventh time, put hands to knees and blow out slowly for seven counts. On the eighth count, stand up sharply, hands on hips and smile for end.

3 Reflect

Cool Down

Ask children to perform their favorite rock song in movement, with no sound. Call out cues to vary the speed and levels. End in a slow motion version on the floor.

9 Irish Social Dance

LESSON AT A GLANCE

Movement Skill Objective Participate in a *ceilidh*-style dance in Sicilian Circle formation, using circling, side gallop, forward-and-back, and star figures, and the pass-through progression

K–4 Dance Standard 5a Perform folk dances from various cultures with competence and confidence

Physical Education Standard 1 Demonstrate competency in movement patterns

MATERIALS
- "St. Patrick Was a Gentleman"
  Teachers' Edition, Gr. 3, p. 290 **CD 10-13**

DANCE SEQUENCE
Intro (8 m.); dance pattern: verse (16 m.) and refrain (8 m.) four times through; coda (8 m.)

DANCE NOTES
- This reel is in meter in 2 and moves at a more sedate pace than some other Irish tunes, making it useful for a first experience with the progressive dance pattern.
- Note that on each of the four times through, the music flows smoothly from the end of the melody immediately into the beginning again, so dancers must be prepared to flow smoothly from the end of the pattern immediately back to the start.

1 Prepare

Background

This is not a traditional Irish dance, but one arranged for this melody, using typical Irish *ceilidh* [cay-lee] dance steps. The *ceilidh* is an Irish and Scottish dance party at which people enjoy social dances in sets of two or more couples. The figures in the pattern are similar to those in square dances of the United States. This is not surprising as the Irish set dance is one of the ancestors of the square dance.

2 Take Action

Formation

Have students take partners and form a circle with couples facing couples, called a **Sicilian circle**. Name the partners *one* and *two* (or tie kerchiefs on the *ones*); *two* is on the right of *one*. Traditionally, men are on the left and women on the right. Students might try it this way also.

SICILIAN CIRCLE

Dance the Verse

Play the Dance Performance recording of "St. Patrick Was a Gentleman" **CD 10-13** and stop it after the first time through the verse. Then teach the first two 8-measure figures without the recording.

- **Figure 1A, measures 1–4**
  Each group or set of four joins hands in a circle with elbows bent in the **W hold**, and then **slides** to the left for 8 beats.

- **Figure 1B, measures 5–8**
  Each set slides to the right for 8 beats.

Teaching Tip—Instead of counting the beats for the students, it is better to sing, hum, *la-la-la*, or doodle the melody, so they will learn to match the movements to the musical phrases, and not merely march to the beat.

- **Figure 2A, measures 9–12**
  Each set makes a **right-hand star** and walks **clockwise** for 8 beats. Grasping wrists is the traditional way, but use whichever style is best for the group.

RIGHT-HAND STAR

Piling hands | Grasping opposite hands | Grasping wrists

- **Figure 2B, measures 13–16**
  Each set makes a **left-hand star** and moves **counterclockwise** for 8 beats.

Now play the recording again and have the class practice the first two figures to the recorded music.

Dance the Refrain

Prepare for this figure by playing the recording of the refrain which starts at the *fermata*, CD counter number 0:30, and then continues for eight measures, ending at counter number 0:41. Then teach the following figures.

- **Figure 3A, measures 17–18**
  The pairs, with inside hands joined, walk toward each other 4 steps.

- **Figure 3B, measures 19–20**
  Each pair moves backward 4 steps.

- **Figure 4, measures 21–24**
  Dropping hands, each pair walks forward to pass by the other pair's right shoulders, progressing through to meet an oncoming couple. Immediately, all four join hands in a W hold, as in Figure 1A, to start the dance pattern again.

Grade 3

Coda and Cool Down

- **Measures 1–2** Bow and say thank you to the partner.
- **Measures 3–4** Bow and say thank you to the one diagonally across.
- **Measures 5–6** Bow and say thank you to the one directly across.
- **Measures 7–8** Wave and say thank you to everyone else.

Dance the Dance

Play the recording and have the class get set in starting position during the 8-measure introduction. Have students perform the verse-and-refrain figures four times in all and end with the Coda and Cool Down.

Observe how well students perform the steps of the figures and the transitions between the figures.

3 Reflect

Discussion

ASK Did everyone pass through all right? Were you ready to circle left when the pattern began again? Did you remember each figure?
(Encourage students to share responses.)

6 1920s Blues Dance

LESSON AT A GLANCE

Movement Skill Objective Move confidently and competently in a blues dance style that includes step-close and step-touch patterns

K–4 Dance Standards 5a Perform folk dances from various cultures with competence and confidence

Physical Education Standard 1 Demonstrate competency in movement patterns

MATERIALS
- "Joe Turner Blues"
  Teachers' Edition, Gr. 4, p. 56   **CD 3-14**

RECORDING ROUTINE
Intro (4 m.), v. 1 (12 m.); v. 2 (12 m.); v. 3 (12 m.)

DANCE NOTE
This is a simple movement pattern, and it may be done to almost any 12-bar blues tune. Like many blues songs, it has cultural, historic, and musical underpinnings that may require students to be somewhat socially and musically sophisticated to appreciate it. Be aware that it is sometimes more difficult to do a slow dance than a fast one.

1 Prepare

Background
Blues dances such as the one presented here emerged in the early jazz era and were popular in the United States between World War I and World War II during the 1920s and 1930s.

Warm Up
Have students sit and listen to "Joe Turner Blues" **CD 3-14**. Discuss what it might be like to have the blues. Encourage them to feel the style, the pulse, and the emotion of the words and music.

2 Take Action

Formation
Students stand scattered around the dance space, each student facing a partner. Partners hold hands in front, about waist high, and then raise them sideways as high as is comfortable for both partners (about shoulder height). This is the **airplane hold**.

The Steps
Measures 1–4 *They* <u>*tell me*</u> *Joe Turner's come and gone.*

- Start on the <u>down beat</u> (underlined lyrics signify the down beat).
- Partners move **CCW, step side-and-close** three times, then **side-and-touch.**
- Arms rock up and down with each beat.

Measures 5–8 *They* <u>*tell me*</u> *Joe Turner's come and gone*

- Move **CW** and repeat the pattern of Measures 1–4.

Measures 9–12 *He* <u>*left me*</u> *here to sing this song.*

- Turning away from each other, partners walk in a full circle in 8 slow steps. They may raise their arms and slowly waggle their hands in the air in the 1920s Charleston style.

Repeat the entire sequence for verses 2 and 3.

Dance the Blues
Play the song recording again and have students perform the entire dance in time with the music. Observe their ability to move confidently and competently through the sequence.

3 Reflect

Cool Down
Partners should nod or bow to each other and say "Thank you, partner."

Discussion
ASK Were you and your partner able to move together to the slow blues beat? How did you like dancing to this type of song? (Encourage them to share their impressions of blues music and dance.)

Grade 4

7 A Ĉárdás from Slovakia

LESSON AT A GLANCE

Movement Skill Objective Learn the Slovak *ĉárdás* step and develop the ability to lead and follow a group in curved pathways

K–4 Dance Standard 5a Perform folk dances from various cultures with competence and confidence

Physical Education Standard 1 Demonstrate competency in movement patterns

MATERIALS

- "*Tancovaĉka*" Teachers' Edition, Gr. 4, p. 230   **CD 9-39, 40, 46**

RECORDING ROUTINE

Intro (8 m.); verse (16 m.); refrain (16 m.); interlude (4 m.); verse (16 m.); refrain (16 m.); coda (4 m.)

DANCE NOTE

- The music is in meter in 2. Watch for the *accelerando* in the last eight measures of the refrain.

1 Prepare

Background

The Slovakian *ĉárdás* [CHAR-dahsh] step is performed and pronounced the same as the Hungarian *csárdás* step. Both figures are related to the *side-close-side-touch* step in many cultures. Note that the word *ĉsárdás* often refers to a type of traditional Hungarian couple dance, which includes this style of step pattern.

Warm Up

Play the recording of "*Tancovaĉka*" **CD 9-39** and have students move in the style of the *ĉárdás* step by walking around the dance space, bending their knees slightly on each step. As they take each step—

SAY Down, down, down.

2 Take Action

Formation

Start in a closed circle, hands in **V hold**, facing center. Choose a student to be the first leader for the refrain; the student to his or her right will be the second leader.

Verse (*ĉárdás* step)

- **Measures 1–4** Side R, close L, side R, close L, side R, close L, side R, touch L. Bend knees slightly on each beat.
- **Measures 5–8** Repeat with opposite footwork in the other direction, ending with a touch on the R foot.
- **Measures 9–16** Repeat *ĉárdás* step to right and left, as above.

SAY Now try the *ĉárdás* step to the practice track with its slower tempo.

Play the Dance Practice Tempo **CD 9-46** and observe students perform the step.

SAY Much better! Here comes the regular tempo in the Slovak language.

Play the Slovak version of the song **CD 9-39** and pause it when the refrain begins.

Refrain (*tra-la-la*/snails and snakes)

- **Measures 17–24** The first leader drops hands with the second leader and winds the group into a snail formation (16 steps).
- **Measures 25–32** The second leader, who is now at the end of the snail, unwinds the group back into a circle.

SAY This is the whole pattern, one time through. Now do all that to the music.

Have students practice with the refrain music.

- **Interlude** Form the circle again and choose two new leaders (8 beats) for the refrain.
- **Measures 1–16** Repeat the verse figure in a closed circle.

SAY In the refrain the new first leader may guide us in a snake or other formations. But the second leader always brings us back into the circle.

- **Measures 17–32** Repeat refrain with the new leaders.

Coda (a traditional ending step)

Everyone takes four strong stomps in place (counts *1-and-2-and*), then jumps on both feet in a crossed position (count *3*), jumps and lands with both feet open a bit to the side (count *and*), slides feet together with a snap (count *4*), and holds (count *and*).

SAY Now repeat the dance with the English version of the song. During the introduction, I will choose new leaders.

Play the English version of the song **CD 9-40** and have students perform the entire dance sequence. Repeat the dance so that all students have a chance to be the first and second leaders.

3 Reflect

Discussion

ASK Were you able to always bend your knees in the *ĉárdás* step? (Students can discuss any difficulty or success they had.)

Did the leaders do a good job of guiding you around? (Allow students to share their ideas but encourage them to be constructive when they give suggestions for improvement.)

LESSON

4 Double-Line Country Dance

LESSON AT A GLANCE

Movement Skill Objective Demonstrate proficiency in line dance patterns while interacting with a partner and others

5–8 Dance Standards 5b Competently perform social dances from a broad spectrum of twentieth-century America

Physical Education Standards 1 Demonstrate competency in movement patterns

MATERIALS
• *I Love a Rainy Night*
Teachers' Edition, Gr. 5, p. 350   **CD 16-9, 10**

RECORDING ROUTINE
Intro (8 m.); v. 1 (8 m.); v. 2 (8 m.); refrain (12 m.); v. 3 (8 m.); v. 4 (8 m.); refrain (12 m.); interlude (8 m.); refrain (32 m.); fade out

DANCE NOTE
The dance pattern repeats 12 times.

Country dances or line dances are popular because they are easy to teach. Upper elementary students enjoy line dances because they do not have to touch anyone. The dance pattern presented here includes those good points, but has additional value because it is done with two people facing and interacting—an important practice for young people today.

1 Prepare

Background

Country music has been popular in the United States since the 1920s, when early radio programs began to broadcast this style. Line dancing, which is often accompanied by country music, is a good place to start for those who still need to be convinced that dancing can be enjoyable.

Warm Up

Play the recording of *I Love a Rainy Night* **CD 16-9** to engage the students and start them feeling the beat. Let them know that the artist is a talented country musician, Eddie Rabbit.

SAY You will want to know who our important artists are—someday you may be one too.

2 Take Action

Teaching Tip

When teaching line dances, you must either

• Face the students who will **mirror** your movements (you will need to remember that your right is their left, and so on), or

• Turn your back to the students (if you have an assistant) and have students imitate your movements.

If these options are not possible, teach the first three figures in a circle formation so that students can see you and you can see them.

Formation

Students should choose partners (it is best, for this dance, to let them choose their own) and stand across from their partners in double lines across the room.

DOUBLE LINE FORMATION

SAY Stretch out your lines so everyone has plenty of elbowroom on both sides.

Start students in double lines as follows.

SAY Please turn toward me to learn the parts. W to move until the vocal begins.

Parts of the Dance

• **Part I, 8 beats, measures 1–2**

Give the Cue: "Out-in"

• Students stand on left foot and perform right heel turns *out-in-out-in-out-in-out-in*.

• **Part 2, 8 beats, measures 3–4**

Give the Cue: "Tapping"

• Still on left foot, right foot taps in front twice, in back twice, in front, in back, to the side, raise right knee up.

SAY Say these words without doing the action. *front, in front, in back, in back, in front, in back, side, up.* Say it again. Now do what you just said.

SAY At first, if you have trouble tapping in the correct places, do not worry about it—it will come. The most important part is getting your right knee up on beat eight.

Instruct students to **practice** several times slowly, using the Dance Practice Tempo **CD 16-10**. Then bring them up to tempo. When they are ready, play the Dance Performance **CD 16-9** for the first two parts several times, pausing the movements (not the recording) for the 16 beats for which no instruction has yet been given.

- **Part 3, 8 beats, measures 5–6**

Give the Cue: "To your own right side"

- Students step right foot to the side (beat 1), close left foot to the right foot (beat 2), right to the side (beat 3), touch left beside right and clap (beat 4).

Give the Cue: "To your left"

- Repeat previous action by starting with the left foot and go the other direction for beats 5-6-7-8.

ASK When you go to your own right, does it look as if your partner is going the same direction or the opposite? (opposite)

SAY If you are going in the wrong direction, it may be because you are not holding up your right knee long enough at the end of Part 2. When you put down your right foot, it should be the first step of Part 3. This is what I mean.

SAY Practice the transition from Part 2 to Part 3. Right knee up, hold one beat. Now step on right foot to the side. Do that again. Do it once more and continue all of Part 3—right knee up, and . . . side-together-side-touch. Good!

Play the Dance Practice Tempo recording to rehearse Parts 2, 3, and then back to 1. If they have been in a circle, this is the time to get students into the double line formation. Now practice what they have learned so far with the Dance Performance recording.

- **Part 4, 8 beats, measures 7–8**

Give the Cue: "Changing places"

- Passing right shoulders, partners cross each other to exchange places and stay there to start the dance again. (This is not a *do-si-do*.)

SAY Use all eight beats—do not race across—and give it a bit of country-dance styling (show them).

Note: Although it is always best to encourage students to listen to musical phrases, it may be necessary to count the beats for those with less experience.

More tips: Do not allow all of the boys to gather in one area and the girls in another. If this happens, rearrange the scene so that competent dancers are interspersed among those who need more help.

SAY If you are not sure what to do, watch the person next to you, not the person across from you.

Encourage students to sing along with the refrain. Playfully "warn" them that this is a powerful song and that it very likely will rain that evening.

The Whole Dance

After some rehearsal of the whole pattern, it is time for the entire dance. Play the Dance Performance recording and have students move through the entire sequence twelve times. You may cue the parts as necessary and help students keep track of how many times they have run through the sequence. Observe how well students remember when to do what action and how well they execute the entire sequence of movements.

3 Reflect

Discussion

ASK How did it go? Were you able remember the pattern and make the transitions to each part? Did you avoid bouncing off of each other? Did you enjoy it? (Allow students to share their experiences and to self-assess their personal performances. Also accept suggestions for improving the class performance.)

———————————

6 Mexican Longways Dance

LESSON AT A GLANCE

Movement Skill Objective With a partner and others, perform a Mexican-style polka step in a longways set

5–8 Dance Standards 5a Competently perform folk dances from various cultures; describe similarities and differences in steps and movement styles

Physical Education Standard 6 Values physical activity for health, enjoyment, challenge, and social interaction

MATERIALS

- *"Asi es mi Tierra"*
  Teachers' Edition, Gr. 6, p. 172   **CD 9-35, 36**
- Costumes for a performance: girls—colorful full skirts and a flower in their hair; boys—*sombreros* hanging down their backs, cowboy boots, and belts with fancy buckles.

MUSIC AND DANCE SEQUENCE

Intro (4 m.); section A.1 (16 m.); section A.2 (16 m.); section B (8 m.); section A.3 (8 m.); A.1 (16 m.); A.2 (16 m.); B (8 m.); A.3 (8 m.); coda (4 m.)

DANCE NOTE

There are two beats to a measure.

This dance is a good introduction to the polka, or two-step, which is popular in northern Mexico as well as in other cultures. Students may be comfortable with this polka because the music moves at a peaceful pace and the pattern does not require the ballroom position. The pattern does require, however, that boys and girls are partners, as is traditional in Mexican social dances. If classroom realities make this difficult, other partner arrangements are acceptable.

1 Prepare

Background

The movements of this adapted pattern are typical of *norteño* dances from both sides of the border of Mexico and the United States. The pattern combines the vigorous style of northern Mexico with steps from the United States and Europe.

Warm Up

Before setting up the formation for this dance, have students practice the **polka step**, using the *"Asi es mi Tierra"* Dance Practice Tempo **CD 9-36**.

2 Take Action

Formation

Students stand across from partners in **longways sets** of 4–6 pairs. Boys have their left (L) shoulders toward the music source, or top of the room, and girls have right (R) shoulders toward music source.

Styling

Girls may hold skirts out at sides and do fancy flourishes or "skirt work;" boys may hook thumbs in their belt buckles or clasp hands behind their backs.

Learn the Dance

Introduction—Girls sway in place while doing skirt work; boys bounce lightly **in place** with thumbs hooked in belt buckles.

Section A.1—Forward and Backward

Note: On the *and* (upbeat) before the first beat of any measure, students lift their heels and then step on the opposite foot. Girls lift on L foot and take first step on R. Boys lift on R foot and take first step on L foot.

- **Measures 1–4** Partners take three **polka steps** toward each other and **stamp.**
- **Measures 5–8** They repeat the three polka steps and stamp moving backward, away from each other.

SAY Wait out the first two notes before starting on the downbeat. Go—*one, two-and-1-2-3-and-2 and-3-2-3-and-stamp-2-3-and-1-2-3-and-2-2-3-and-3-2-3-and-stamp-2-3.*

SAY If you are not comfortable with the polka step, forget the lift and do the **two-step.**

Note: Students who cannot do the two-step may walk seven steps and stamp forward, then backward.

- **Measures 9–16** Repeat measures 1–8, for and then backward.

At this point, play the Dance Performance **CD 9-35** so that students can practice this section of the pattern.

Section A.2—Exchanging Partners

- **Measures 1–4** The top boy takes both his partner's hands and travels to the foot of the set in eight **sashay steps**. He leaves her there at the bottom or below the last girl.
- **Measures 5–8** The same boy joins two hands with the bottom girl and takes her up to the top in eight sashay steps, leaving her in the first spot.
- **Measures 9–12** The bottom boy takes the former top girl, who is now in the last spot, back to the top of the set in eight sashay steps, leaving her above the former last girl who is now in the top spot.
- **Measures 13–16** The same (bottom) boy takes his first partner back to her original spot at the bottom of the set. (Students shift to fill empty spots.)

At this point, have students practice sections A.1 and A.2 to music.

Section B (8 m.)—Elbow Turns

Everyone should do **R-elbow turns** for four polka steps, then L-elbow turns for four polka steps.

Play the A.1, A.2, and B sections of the music so that students may practice the patterns and transitions.

Grade 6

Section A.3 (16 m.)—Cast Off and Do-si-do

The top pair in each set **casts off** to the bottom of the set with eight polka steps or two-steps (or sixteen walking steps).

At the same time, the other pairs do a R-shoulder **do-si-do** in four polka steps or two-steps (or eight walking steps). Repeat with L shoulders. They shift positions so that the second couple becomes the top couple to begin the dance again. Allow the second pair to practice it on the second time through the sequence.

Coda

Except for the last time through, partners should sway and bounce as in the Introduction. On the final Coda, they bow dramatically to each other. Then with one hand on the waist, fling up the other while stamping one foot.

Dance the Dance

Give every pair a chance to be the top couple. As the recording goes through the entire sequence only twice, set the CD player to auto repeat so that the music will repeat as many times as necessary. Observe how well students execute the polka step with Mexican styling.

3 Reflect

Discussion

Ask students to describe their experience of this dance.

ASK Do you feel that you were able to do the polka step confidently and competently? Did your longways-set members work as a team?

SAY Describe how the *norteño* pattern and style is the same and different from traditional dances of the United States that use this formation.

4 Disco Dance

LESSON AT A GLANCE

Movement Skill Objective   Learn moves to a disco dance, including the four-wall turn

5–8 Dance Standard 5b   Competently perform social dances from a broad spectrum of twentieth-century America

Physical Education Standard 1   Demonstrate competency in movement patterns

MATERIALS
- *I Will Survive*
  Teachers' Edition, Gr. 7, p. B-10   **CD 2-14**

RECORDING ROUTINE

Intro (free piano arpeggios); opening vocal (8 m.); v.1 (8 m.); v. 2 (8 m.); refrain (8 m.); v. 3 (8 m.); v. 4 (8 m.); v. 5 (8 m.); refrain (8 m. with fermata at 2:30); v. 6. (8 m.); refrain (8 m.) fade out

DANCE NOTE

This is one of the most popular patterns for the hustle line dance. It is a 10-measure pattern and, as is true with many early disco dances, it does not fit the 8-measure melody.

1 Prepare

Background

The driving beat of *disco* music inspired a new dance style that became a worldwide craze after John Travolta showed his moves in the 1977 film *Saturday Night Fever*. The hustle line dance, sometimes called the "California Hustle" to differentiate it from the partner hustle, is one of the most familiar of the disco dances.

2 Take Action

Formation

A **line dance** with students scattered around the space or in loose lines across the room, all facing the same direction.

Learn the Hustle

Begin the dance after the introduction and 8-measure opening vocal (where the driving beat starts).

The Steps

- **Measures 1–2 Cue:** "Start on R foot, moving backward"
  Back-2-3-touch L, forward-2-3-touch R.

- **Measures 3–4 Cue:** "Turns"
  Full turn in four counts R-L-R-touch L, L-R-L-touch R.

SAY Clap each time you touch your foot.

- **Measure 5 Cue:** "Kick, ball-change" ♪♪♩
  Sharp low kick with R, step on ball of R foot, step on L foot, hold.
  Repeat exactly.

- **Measure 6 Cue:** "Twists and points"
  Twisting torso slightly to R, bend R knee while stepping on R foot and point R index finger down to R; repeat to L with L foot and L finger point.
  Repeat to R and L (4 beats).

SAY Before continuing we will do all that with the music. Now, first two rows go to the back and all others move up please.

- **Measure 7 Cue:** "John Travolta pointing figure"
  With L hand on hip, point R index finger to high R corner; bring down same finger and point it at L hip. Repeat these points.

(Some disco teachers call this "pistol, holster holster," but let's not.)

- **Measure 8 Cue:** "Roll, roll, click, click"
  Roll hands in front twice, click heels twice.

- **Measures 9–10 Cue:** "Toe taps quarter turn to left"
  With R foot tap 2 times in front, 2 times in back (4 beats), in front (beat 1), in back (beat 2), to side (beat 3), and pull up R knee sharply (beat 4).

Tip: Do not show the quarter turn until students are comfortable with the entire pattern. At this point play the recording of *I Will Survive* **CD 2-14** to rehearse the ten measures enough times until most students have it.

SAY This pattern actually ends facing another wall. That is why it is called a **four-wall dance**. The next wall is to the left. Identify it as the second wall.

SAY Continuing left, turn to the third wall, and finally turn to the fourth wall before starting again at the first wall. Show me the walls again.

SAY Here is how we turn as the pattern ends—At the first wall bring up your R knee, **pivot** on L foot to move a quarter turn L to face the second wall. T that. Good! Now do the toe taps with the turn to the third wall and now the last wall.

SAY Okay, first two rows go to the back and all others move up, please. Now I think you are ready for the whole dance!

Do the Hustle

Play the recording and have students do the hustle line dance. Observe their ability to competently and accurately move in the given sequence with the music.

3 Reflect

Discussion

Lead a discussion where students assess their own dance skills.

ASK Were you able to pivot on the beat when turning to the next wall? Did you face in the correct direction each time? What did you think of this song?

Grade 7

5 A Greek Dance

LESSON AT A GLANCE

Movement Skill Objective Comfortably use the T hold and accurately demonstrate the style of a traditional Greek dance

5–8 Dance Standard 5a Competently perform folk dances from various cultures

Physical Education Standard 1 Demonstrate competency in motor skills and movement patterns

MATERIALS
- *Stalia, Stalia*
  Teachers' Edition, Gr. 8, p. B-21   **CD 3-3**

DANCE SEQUENCE

Section	Movement
Intro (2 m.)	Listen
Music (24 m./3 sets of 8 m.)	Dance 4-part sequence 3 times though
Interlude (2 m.)	Dance part 1
Music (40 m./5 sets of 8 m.)	Dance 4-part sequence 5 times through

DANCE NOTES

There are four beats to each measure in this music.

As is common in many Greek dances, the leader may improvise steps while keeping the basic rhythm. The pattern presented here is a base from which to improvise.

1 Prepare

Background

Dancing is very much a part of Greek life. Many of the dances done today came from ancient times. This traditional *Varis* (slow) *Hasapikos* [hah-SAH-pee-kohs] is similar to the *Syrtaki* [sir-TAH-kee], a dance that became more popular after the film *Zorba the Greek*.

Warm Up

Students should get comfortable with the style of this music before learning the pattern. Play the recording of *Stalia, Stalia* **CD 3-3**. While sitting, have students sway and clap on the heavy beat, then rise to take slow, deliberate steps around the room, clapping on the off-beat and focusing on the music.

2 Take Action

Formation

Short lines of 3 to 6 people in the **T hold**. The person on the right end is the leader. Those on either end hold their free arms out to the side. While learning the pattern, students may dance independently or use the **V hold**. All face center.

Hasapikos Steps

Practice the steps before dancing with the music.

- **Part 1**
  Measures 1–2 Step sideways on R foot (counts 1-2), close L to R (counts 3-4); repeat with L to side (counts 5-6), close R (counts 7-8).

- **Part 2**
  Measures 3–4 Rock back on heels, opening feet in V shape (counts 1-2), lean forward on toes, opening heels (counts 3-4), lean forward on toes, closing heels (counts 5-6), rock back on heels, closing feet (counts 7-8).

- **Part 3**
  Measures 5–6 Step or small leap forward onto L foot with knees slightly bent, R foot extended in back (count 1). Touch R toe in back (count 2). Brush R foot forward (count 3). Lift R leg forward (count 4). Step back on R (count 5). Lift L knee and lean back a bit (count 6). Step back on L (count 7). Lift R knee and lean back a bit (count 8).

- **Part 4**
  Measures 7–8 Step across on R (in front of) L (count 1), small step side on L (count 2), step on R across L (count 3), small step side on L (count 4), step on R across L (count 5), strong step side on L (count 6), close R to L (count 7), hold (count 8).

SAY After you do this 4-part sequence three times, listen for the 2-measure interlude and perform part 1 (side-and-close-and-side-and-close).

Note: After the interlude, perform the sequence five times through, starting with part 1.

Dance the *Hasapikos*

Play the recording and invite students to dance. Begin to move after the 2-measure (8 beats) introduction. Observe how well they accomplish the footwork while maintaining the T hold in their lines.

3 Reflect

Discussion

ASK Were you comfortable with the T hold position? (Allow students to talk about their experience with the dance.)

What other steps could we add to this pattern? (Encourage appropriate suggestions and try them out.)

Option: Invite volunteer line leaders to improvise with alternate steps suggested by the class while others in the line follow along.

Creative Movement

What Is Creative Movement?

Creative Movement offers students the opportunity to invent choreography by using self-generated movements that coordinate with a variety of evocative musical selections. A carefully designed lesson structure, based on a specific choreographic concept, aids teachers in facilitating this process. The pool of ideas about which a dance can be made is virtually limitless. The pleasure of one's own imagination, guided within the world of dance, provides a wonderful opportunity for students to create, observe, and reflect. Here, students build upon skills to create movement studies that they can share with their classmates.

Creative movement uses techniques and skills that students developed in Movement Basics as the instruments with which they create choreography. Activities in each lesson help ensure that students exaggerate and abstract movement, making a clear distinction between normal everyday movement and creative dance movement.

The sequence at all grade levels contains a consistent set of five lessons, plus a set of lessons that are built on thematic and conceptual choreographic variables.

The five consistent lessons are designed so that students generate movement based on the following

- Celebrations • use of props • sports-generated movement • the spoken word • verb lists

Thematic choices may be generated by ideas such as

- Emotions • character studies • the environment • animal movements • the elements

Choreographic concepts to be explored include

- Geometric body shapes • pathways • negative and positive space • partnerships • canon • dynamics

Music and recorded poetry play integral roles in providing an atmosphere for creativity in dance and movement. Each lesson is carefully constructed to marry the form and feel of the music or spoken word with the content and goal of the choreographic concept. Recorded selections range from contemporary rock 'n' roll, classical and contemporary art music, jazz, poetry, to world music. All lessons are created so that the activity can be successfully completed within one class session.

2 Birds Flying and Landing

LESSON AT A GLANCE

Movement Skill Objective   Create a bird dance using axial movements that change levels

K–4 Dance Standard 1c   Create shapes at low, middle, and high levels

Physical Education Standard 2   Demonstrate understanding of movement concepts as they apply to the performance of physical activities

MATERIALS
- *Bird*
  Teacher's Edition, Gr. 1, p. 39

DANCE NOTES
Use the sound of the music to help create the environment of a peaceful gathering place for birds. You may wish to use the auto repeat function on your CD player.

1 Prepare

Background
Talk about various types of birds and how they fly

ASK Do the wings move fast or slow? Do they glide? Are the moves choppy or smooth? children to demonstrate flapping gestures.)

2 Take Action

Formation
Groups of three to six children, gathered in spots around the space.

SAY We are in a peaceful place where birds like to gather.

Create a Bird Dance
Play the recording of *Bird* **CD 2-3** and have all children create **stationary** bird actions. Then each group go for a bird flight and landing. As the other groups wait their turns, have them imagine that they are "resting" birds. If space is limited, or children are unsure of where to go, have them travel in a circle around the outside of the other groupings.

SAY At the end of your flight, think about how your bird would land.

3 Reflect

Cool Down
In silence, invite the children to become beautiful giant water birds. Have them balance on one leg for as long as they can. When balance has been achieved, have each child sit still in the form of a floating water bird.

SAY Hold your muscles still. Let your bird blend into its surroundings.

3 Baseball Boogie

LESSON AT A GLANCE

Movement Skill Objective   Create a dance based on movements used in sports

K–4 Dance Standard 2b   Improvise, create, and perform dances based on their own ideas and concepts from other sources

Physical Education Standard 5   Exhibit responsible personal and social behavior in physical activity settings

MATERIALS

- *The Stars and Stripes Forever*
  Teacher's Edition, Gr. 1, p. 167   **CD 5-28**

DANCE COUNT SEQUENCE

Count in sets of eight at a march tempo.

Section	Count	Action
Intro	8 counts	Rub hands
Section A	4 sets of 8	At bat
Section B	4 sets of 8	Pitching
Section C	4 sets of 8	Outfield catching
Section D	4 sets of 8	Running bases
Section E	4 sets of 8	Catcher
Section F	4 sets of 8	Umpire
Section G	6 sets of 8	Strike out
Section H	8 sets of 8 (piccolos)	Favorite baseball moves
Section I	6 sets of 8 (trombones)	Silent crowd cheers
Coda	8 sets of 8	Home run hitters

1 Prepare

Warm Up

Have the children create a verbal list of six actions used in baseball. In slow motion and remaining **stationary**, have the children recreate each action with as much detail and authenticity as they can.

ASK How real can you make your moves?

2 Take Action

Formation

Children stand in a stationary grid.

Baseball Boogie Dance

Using the Dance Count Sequence in the Lesson at a Glance, have each child improvise his or her own baseball dance. Encourage the children to think of themselves as baseball comedians. Play the recording of *The Stars and Stripes Forever* **CD 5-28.** Coach the children through the music and the Dance Count Sequence by announcing the moves in the voice of a baseball announcer. Remind the children to stay in their own spots as they move, but encourage them to **jump,** kneel, **stretch**, and **slide.**

Children do not need to remember patterns but should improvise appropriate movements based on the announcer's cues. After practicing as an entire ensemble a few times, divide the class into two groups—"baseball boogie dancers" and the "stadium crowd."

Have the stadium crowd watch the baseball boogie dancers and choose one move by one dancer that they like the best. The stadium crowd children can mime eating peanuts or hot dogs while they watch the dancers perform.

SAY Stadium crowd, show us the move you liked the best.

Switch roles so that all children have a chance to dance.

3 Reflect

Cool Down

With the children standing in a circle, play catch with a pretend ball.

SAY Make sure we can tell what kind of ball you are throwing. Do not drop the ball!

LESSON 5 — The Cookie Factory

LESSON AT A GLANCE

Movement Skill Objective Maintain personal space while creating movement sequences

K–4 Dance Standard 1d Demonstrate the ability to define and maintain personal space

Physical Education Standard 5 Exhibit responsible personal and social behavior that respects self and others in physical activity settings

MATERIALS
- *Arirang*
  Teacher's Edition, Gr. 2, p. 137   **CD 5-29**

DANCE NOTES
It is advisable that you use the auto repeat function on your CD player.

1 Prepare

Warm Up
Have the children sit in a circle and create and pass hand gestures around the circle.

2 Take Action
With the children standing in a large circle, play the recording of *Arirang* **CD 5-29.** Invite the children to imagine that they are each a small moving part of a giant factory.

Cookie Factory Dance
Have the children begin moving **counterclockwise** in the circle. Maintain the size of the circle and the spacing between the children. Children move like various mechanical parts in the factory.

SAY Let the music tell your body what to do.

After one rotation, reverse direction and go **clockwise** for another complete rotation. Then all children stop and move in stationary position. As the music continues, **cue** each child to enter the center of circle one at a time. Each child chooses a spot in the center of the circle and continues to move. Children in the outer circle continue moving also.

SAY Go under, over, or inside the other parts of the machine. Do not touch other machine parts.

When all the children have joined the factory, fade out the music and have them freeze.

SAY It is time to turn off the machine.

3 Reflect

Discussion
Talk about the children's cookie-making machine.

ASK What part of the cookie-making process did your machine part perform? (Allow the children to share answers.)

LESSON 8 — Boogie to the Words

LESSON AT A GLANCE

Movement Skill Objective Use axial movements to create a dance that coordinates with a speech piece

K–4 Dance Standard 1a Accurately demonstrate nonlocomotor/axial movements (such as bend, twist, stretch, swing)

Physical Education Standard 1 Demonstrate competency in motor skills needed to perform a variety of physical activities

MATERIALS
- "Boogie Chant and Dance"
  Teacher's Edition, Gr. 2, p. 78

RECORDING ROUTINE
- Intro (4 m.); vocal phrase 1 (4 m.); vocal phrase 2 (7 m.); vocal phrase 3 (10 m.); coda (2 m.)

DANCE NOTE
Each measure has four beats.

1 Prepare

Warm Up
As the children are rising from their chairs to stand, pretend that a balloon is falling from the sky. Ask them to help you keep the balloon in the air by stretching to push the balloon upward, **swinging twisting** when the balloon falls to the side; **bending** as the balloon falls to the ground to push it up to the sky.

SAY Please stand and help me keep the balloon from falling to the ground; stretch to push it upward, twist and reach out to the side and lift it upward, then bend down to pick it up.

2 Take Action

Formation
The movements for this activity are **stationar** children stand in grid formation leaving enough space so that they can stretch upward and outward.

SAY Be sure you can move freely without touching any of the other children.

Practice Moving in a Sequence
Ask children to **mirror** these movements while you count out loud.

- **Introduction**—Bop head to the beat, hands on hips (8 beats).
- **Vocal Phrase 1**—Bend at the waist (2 beats) and rise (2 beats), four times.
- **Vocal Phrase 2**—Twist L at the waist (2 beats), twist R (2 beats), three times. Bend to the floor and bend the knees to the beat (8 beats). Shake shoulders while rising and falling toward the floor (8 beats).

- **Vocal Phrase 3**—Stretch arms up (8 beats) and bend down (8 beats). Sway from side to side (3 sets of 8 beats).
- **Coda**—Stand still, heads bowed (7 beats), then throw hands in the air on beat 8.

Moving with Music

Play the recording of "Boogie Chant and Dance" **CD 3-22**. Ask children to perform the movements they just practiced with the music.

Creating New Moves

Let the children know that it is time to invent new movements to go with the vocal phrases. Play the recording phrase by phrase and let the children experiment with various movements. Remind them that they should remain **in place** while they move in order to avoid collisions.

Then invite volunteers to demonstrate movements that go with particular sentences in the speech piece such as *Got a nickel, buy a pickle*. Have the rest of the class mirror those movements. Allow the class to choose their favorite new moves to incorporate into the dance sequence.

Practice the dance sequence with the new movements and then play the recording to accompany the dance. You may wish to use the auto repeat function on your CD player so that the children can perform the dance several times in a row.

3 Reflect

Cool Down

Have the children slowly stretch their arms upward and downward. Ask them to stretch their bodies upward and then down to the floor and slowly lie down.

Fireworks

LESSON AT A GLANCE

Movement Skill Objective   Create a dance sequence based on the theme of fireworks using increasingly complex movements at various levels

K–4 Dance Standard 1c   Create shapes at low, medium, and high levels

Physical Education Standard 6   Value physical activity for enjoyment and self-expression

MATERIALS
- *Fontane di Roma,* "*La fontana di Trevi al meriggio*" Teacher's Edition, Gr. 2, p. 92   **CD 3-52**

DANCE NOTE

Children should listen for musical events to inspire their fireworks movements.

1 Prepare

Warm Up

Standing in neutral position children melt to the floor while counting backwards slowly from eight to zero. Rewind from zero to eight and end by standing in neutral position. Repeat a few times.

2 Take Action

Have each child develop a sequence of **stationary** moves that begin at the low level, proceed up through the middle and high levels, and end back at the low level. Then, using the theme of *fireworks,* have the children add expressive elements to their sequences and explode at the top. After the explosion at the top, children float back to a low level.

SAY Visualize your favorite type of fireworks.

ASK Do they twist and turn? How high can your fireworks go?

Play the recording of *Fontane di Roma* **CD 3-52**.

SAY Listen for sounds that will help your fireworks explode.

After experimenting a number of times with simple moves, encourage the children to develop more complex shapes, twists, bends, and turns.

ASK On the way down, do your fireworks fizzle, float, or spatter?

Once the fireworks dance is created and set, encourage the children to add body percussion sounds as they move.

3 Reflect

Discussion

Invite the children to describe their own fireworks dances, using descriptive adjectives. Encourage them to be creative in their choice of words. Allow them to name their dances.

1 Time and Motion

LESSON AT A GLANCE

Movement Skill Objective   Invent a movement sequence that responds to the beat and tempo changes in music

K–4 Dance Standard 1f   Demonstrate accuracy in moving to a musical beat and responding to changes in tempo

Physical Education Standard 6   Value physical activity for enjoyment, challenge, and self-expression

MATERIALS

* *Gavotte*
  Teacher's Edition, Gr. 3, p. 88   **CD 3-22**

DANCE COUNT SEQUENCE

Section	Music Cue/Movement	Count
Section A1	*Staccato,* unison	4 sets of 8
Section A2	*Staccato,* unison	4 sets of 8
Section B1	Legs and torsos	4 sets of 8
Section C1	*Legato,* change levels	4 sets of 8
Section C2	*Legato,* change levels	4 sets of 8
Section D	*Legato* & *staccato,* contrast	4 sets of 8
Section A3	*Staccato* tones, unison	4 sets of 8
Section B2	Legs and torsos	4 sets of 8

1 Prepare

Warm Up

With the class seated, have each student create a 4-count arm movement sequence. Repeat the pattern a number of times, varying the speed and the quality of the movements.

SAY Perform the movements really fast, ten times in a row. Then change the feel of the movements from very sharp to very smooth.

2 Take Action

Formation

Have students find **home spots** and remain **stationary.**

Inventing Movements for the Music

Play the recording of *Gavotte* **CD 3-22.** Have students invent movements based on the rhythm and expressive quality of the music. Encourage them to invent different sequences for each music section described under Dance Count Sequence.

* **Sections A1, A2, A3**—Guide students to share the movements they invented for the A sections of the music. As a group, choose movements and put them in a sequence to be performed in unison by the entire group for Sections A1, A2, and A3.

SAY Let's borrow moves from several different **choreographers.**

SAY Think of ways to help yourself remember the exact sequence of moves.

* **Sections B1 and B2**—Have each student create a repeatable pattern. Encourage students to use their legs, torsos, and arms to invent rhythmic moves.

SAY Move your legs as if they were your arms.

ASK How much motion can you put into your torso? (Students share answers by demonstrating.)

* **Sections C1 and C2**—Have students move at the slowest tempo they can discern in the music. Use this section to change levels as well as tempo. Invite students to invent different shapes and movements that use the floor as a base.

SAY Remember that you must be able to repeat your sequence. Each section has four sets of eight.

ASK How can you move in an interesting way keeping the beat, and staying off your feet? (Students share answers by demonstrating.)

* **Section D**—Students create movements that are very different from the other sections of the dance. Students should remain stationar use changes in level or movement quality spins, or balance to create contrast.

SAY Use the beat but change the feel.

SAY Think about contrast. Now, do not think. Let your body move into contrasting shapes. Move, do not think.

Perform the Dance

Now play the music again and have the class perform the complete dance in sequence. Help them by calling out section letters if necessar

3 Reflect

Cool Down

Use the arm movement sequence from the W Up and have each student create a full body version within the 4-count structure. Repeat the full body version four times, getting slower each time.

SAY Allow the tempo of your movements to get slower and slower until there is no movement.

Grade 3

7 Every Which Way But Up and Down

LESSON AT A GLANCE

Movement Skill Objective   Work in teams to create locomotor pathways, using different foot patterns, directions, and speeds

K–4 Dance Standard 1b   Demonstrate basic locomotor movements traveling forward, backward, sideward, and turning

Physical Education Standard 1   Demonstrate competency in motor skills and movement patterns

MATERIALS
- *Ennanga, "Movement 3"*
  Teacher's Edition, Gr. 3, p. 127   **CD 4-34**

DANCE COUNT SEQUENCE

Section	Music Cue	Count
Section 1	Harp, 18 slow arpeggios	rhythmically free
Section 2	Strings, upbeat	4 sets of 8
Section 3	Strings with piano	4 sets of 8
Section 4	Harp, metric and upbeat	4 sets of 8
Section 5	Piano alternates with strings every 8 counts	4 sets of 8
Section 6	Strings	4 sets of 8
Section 7	Piano alternates with strings every 8 counts	4 sets of 8
Section 8	Harp	2 sets of 8 then 2 chords
Section 9	Harp slow coda	5 slow then 4 slower counts

1 Prepare

Warm Up

Play the recording of *Ennanga, "Movement 3"* **CD 4-34** and have students individually travel **forward**, **backward**, and **sideward**, changing direction when they hear the music sections change. Have students stop moving when the music stops.

2 Take Action

Formation

Arrange the class into groups of three to six students. Each group will **travel** in a line in follow-the-leader formation. Students on either end of the line may lead, depending on the direction in which the group is traveling. Use the nine sections of music described under the Dance Count Sequence above and instruct students to develop nine distinct patterns for traveling forward, backward, and sideward.

Creating Movement Sequences

Groups should create patterns that change when the music sections change. As each group develops its **locomotor** step pattern, they must also create floor **pathways** and keep the sequence consistent.

SAY Use 8-count phrases and repeat the phrases through the music sections.

SAY Remember that you can move slowly or quickly, the choice is yours.

Each group must be able to eventually repeat exactly its step patterns along the pathways. Each group must travel, at least one time each, forward, backward, and sideward. Give suggestions as they work, such as

SAY Try a spin for a change of direction move.

SAY Use muscle memory to help capture your movement ideas.

Encourage each group to design a change of direction move that contrasts the pattern they have been doing. Students can think of these moves as punctuation in grammar or dynamic markings in music. Suggest any of the following.

SAY Try a sudden stop for a change of direction.

SAY Use an unexpected arm, head, or torso move for a change of direction.

For Sections 1 and 9 the entire class may want to work as a team to design a strong beginning and a strong ending for the dance.

SAY Use the slow tempo in Sections 1 and 9 to get ideas for your moves.

The groups may assemble and then disperse during these sections. Encourage students to create a distinct flavor for these sections.

Performance

Play the recording of *Ennanga, "Movement 3"* again and have the groups perform their movement sequences simultaneously. Observe how consistently they perform the steps they created and how well the groups keep to their own pathways without interfering with the pathways of other groups. Observe also whether all movement criteria have been met.

3 Reflect

Cool Down

Moving in silence, have students recreate in moderately slow motion their version of the dance by creating individual pathways. Have students concentrate on maintaining their own space. Suggest that they move in a dream-like variation of the dance. Silently signal when to stop moving and have all dancers sink to a low level. Pause in silence.

Discussion

Encourage students to talk about how they came up with ideas for their movements. Discuss with them what it was like to work in a team to create the movement sequence.

4 Verb Dance

LESSON AT A GLANCE

Movement Skill Objective Invent traveling dance sequences inspired by verbs

K–4 Dance Standard 1b Accurately demonstrate basic locomotor movements (such as walk, run, hop, jump, leap, gallop, slide, and skip), traveling forward, backward, sideward, diagonally, and turning

Physical Education Standard 2 Demonstrate understanding of movement concepts as they apply to the performance of physical activities

MATERIALS

• *Acadian Songs,* "Walking Song"
  Teacher's Edition, Gr. 4, p. 347   **CD 15-9**

DANCE COUNT SEQUENCE

Section	Count
Section A	4 sets of 16
Section B	2 sets of 8 + 2
Section C	5 sets of 16

DANCE NOTE

Make sure that students attend to the tempo changes in the music as they move.

1 Prepare

Warm Up

Have students experiment with basic **locomotor** movements, such as **walk, run, hop, jump, leap, gallop, slide,** and **skip.** As they work with these locomotor movements, encourage students to be aware of the other movers in the space.

SAY Move sideward, and backward, and forward, with the same step. Then perform the movements at slow, medium, and fast tempos.

2 Take Action

Formation

Have students establish home spots and individual pathways.

Creating Dance with Verbs

Use the following pairs of verbs to inspire creative movement.

- Bounce and bend
- Dart and duck
- Take off and topple

Play the recording of *Acadian Songs,* "Walking Song" **CD 15-9.** Have students combine the first pair of verbs with basic locomotor moves to create specific and repeatable movement sequences. Use the word *bounce* to create locomotor movements for Sections A and C of the music. Create **stationary** movements for Section B, using the second word *bend.*

ASK As you combine your movements with the words, what goes into your brain and out through your body? (Let students show you.)

Repeat the music two more times and create two more sequences of repeatable movements with the verb pairs *dart and duck* and *take off and topple.*

ASK How many different ways can you move when you are stationary? (Have a few students demonstrate.)

SAY Try doing your traveling steps **in place** changing **levels.**

Play the music again and use the auto repeat function on the CD player. Allow the recording to play three times through while students perform their verb dances. Observe students' inventiveness in combining the pairs of verbs with basic locomotor movements to create their dances.

3 Reflect

Discussion

SAY Think of things you see happening around you every day.

Create three new lists of verbs, one list beginning with the letter B, one with the letter D, and one with the letter T. Encourage students to mentally invent movement sequences for those verbs.

---

5 Painting and Floating

LESSON AT A GLANCE

Movement Skill Objective Perform nonlocomotor and axial movements to creatively fill a given amount personal space

K–4 Dance Standard 1a Accurately demonstrate nonloco-motor/axial movements, such as bend, twist, and stretch

Physical Education Standard 1 Demonstrate competency in motor skills needed to perform a variety of physical activities

MATERIALS
- *Pulcinella Suite*, "Serenata" Teacher's Edition, Gr. 4, p. 70   **CD 4-3**

DANCE NOTE
Have students use the music to create an atmosphere in which they can paint.

1 Prepare

Background

Describe to students that an axis is a line running through a rotating object. Let them know that they will be the axis of a globe today.

Warm Up

Have students stand and stretch arms upward, downward, and sideward. Then twist back and forth slowly at the waist. Direct them to notice how their muscles feel as they stretch.

2 Take Action

Formation

Direct each student to work in his or her own personal space. All students participate simultaneously facing whatever direction they choose.

SAY Imagine that you are floating inside a giant balloon.

Creating an Environment

Play the recording of Igor Stravinsky's "*Serenata*" from *Pulcinella Suite* **CD 4-3.** Have students imagine that they are painting the entire inside of the balloon with soft smooth strokes and beautiful colors.

ASK Is your brush wide or pointy? Do you want to paint a lot or just a bit of the space? (Allow their actions to be their responses.)

Suggest that first they paint with their fingertips, then with the palms of their hands, the tops of their heads, the bottoms of their feet, their knees, and their hips.

SAY Imagine that you are the axis inside a giant globe. To paint the hard-to-reach spots, you can **twist, turn,** reach, **stretch, bend,** and rotate. Remember that the globe will rotate in reaction to the way that you move.

When the music ends have everyone stand still.

SAY Everyone close your paint cans.

Direct students to call upon muscle memory to loosely recreate their floating movements. Encourage them to use the cadences in the music to pause. The music is written in compound meter and is performed rather *legato,* or smoothly, with subtle changes in dynamics.

Play the music again so that students can identify the cadences at the end of phrases and think about where they might add interesting pauses in their movement sequences.

SAY Let the music help you move. Think about pausing the movement, rather than creating a shape.

Set your CD player to auto repeat. Play the record-ing and direct students to listen for and identify where the music begins again. Then have them loosely recreate their movement sequences, concen-trating on showing mood with a smooth quality of movement and pausing at the cadences.

3 Reflect

Discussion

Observe the variety of axial movement used by the students. Notice how well they keep their balance as they move. Invite them to share about the experience of being an axis inside an imaginary object.

LESSON

6 Where Did My Feet Go?

LESSON AT A GLANCE

Movement Skill Objective Create and memorize complex spatial pathways

5–8 Dance Standard 1g Demonstrate accurate memorization and reproduction of movement sequences

Physical Education Standard 6 Value physical activity for enjoyment, challenge, and self-expression

MATERIALS

• *Brandenburg Concerto No. 4, "Allegro"* (excerpt) Teacher's Edition, Gr. 5, p. 111 **CD 6-2**

• **Props:** small cones, or substitutes for cones such as notebooks, shoes, or book bags

DANCE NOTE

Use the sound of the music to help the students propel themselves through space. If possible, use the auto repeat function on your CD player so that the music will play continuously.

1 Prepare

Warm Up

Working in silence, have students walk through the space without touching anyone else. Call out cues such as *straight, curved, squiggly,* and *jagged* to indicate what kind of pathway the students should explore.

SAY Let your feet make pathways on the floor.

2 Take Action

Formation

Students stand, spread around room with space enough to allow for traveling on individual pathways.

Props

Place small cones around the space (notebooks, shoes, or book bags can be substituted for the cones.)

Working individually, ask students to create complex pathways that they will be able to reproduce exactly. Students should use fairly simple steps and use the props placed around the space to help them build their pathway dance. See diagram above right.

CONE SETUP SHOWING POSSIBLE PATHWA

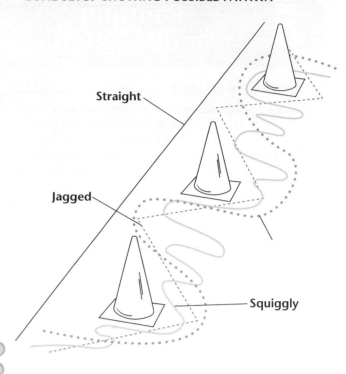

SAY Determine how you will use the props to help you remember your pathway.

Once students are confident that they will be able to remember their pathways, remove the props and ask them to perform the pathway dances without using the props as memory helpers.

Perform the Sequences

Invite them to perform the pathways in groups of five or six students. Repeat the sequences exactly Have other students observe and notice where dancers are not consistent. Have the observers offer constructive suggestions for improvement.

3 Reflect

Cool Down

Have students stand in neutral position and remain stationary.

SAY Without traveling, recreate your pathway dances by using only your arms.

8 Photo Poem

LESSON AT A GLANCE

Movement Skill Objective   Use poetry to generate a simple freeze-frame dance

5–8 Dance Standard 1e   Identify and clearly demonstrate a range of movement qualities

Physical Education Standard 2   Demonstrate understanding of movement concepts as they apply to the performance of physical activities

MATERIALS

• *Stopping by Woods on a Snowy Evening* (Poem)
Teacher's Edition, Gr. 6, p. 40   **CD 2-36**

1 Prepare

Warm Up

Listen to the recording of the poem *Stopping by Woods on a Snowy Evening* **CD 2-36** four times. Encourage students to memorize the poem, or certain phrases of it, after four hearings.

2 Take Action

Creating Shapes

Use the recording to provide a background for the students' movement sequences. Ask each student to create his or own series of positions or shapes, like a short sequence of freeze-frame photos. Students must create at least three shapes that change consistently on a particular word. Students can change their frames as many times as they like, as long as they can reproduce the sequences accurately.

SAY Do not act out the poem. Create moves that look and feel as if someone is watching something, thinking about things, listening, or reacting to something.

Freeze Frame Sequence

Encourage students to exaggerate their shapes or moves, and at the same time maintain the central images of watching, thinking, listening, and reacting. Students may vary the level, the direction they are facing, and the speed with which they change their freeze frames.

SAY As you listen and move, think of yourself as the photographer and show how you feel about what you see. Then <u>be</u> the image in the photograph.

ASK How will your movements or shapes be different?

FREEZE-FRAME SEQUENCE

Watching

Thinking

Reacting

Listening

3 Reflect

Discussion

Talk about the poem and allow students to share the feelings it evoked in them.

Grade 6

3 Walkin' the Walk

LESSON AT A GLANCE

Movement Skill Objective   Improvise a dance, using basic clogging steps in freestyle

5–8 Dance Standard 1b   Accurately demonstrate basic dance steps, positions, and patterns for dance from different styles or traditions

Physical Education Standard 6   Value physical activity for health, enjoyment, challenge, self-expression, and social interaction

MATERIALS
- *Why Walk When You Can Fly?*
  Teacher's Edition, Gr. 7, p. B-28   **CD 4-8**
- Optional: tap shoes; if not available, jingle taps can be glued onto the toes and heels of sneakers with sneaker adhesive

DANCE COUNT SEQUENCE
Count in moderate sets of two.

Section	Music Cue	Count/time
Intro	Slow and free solo piano	0:00–0:51
Section A	Vocal	16 sets of 2
Section B	Instrumental	16 sets of 2
Section A	Vocal	16 sets of 2
Section B	Instrumental	16 sets of 2
Section A	Vocal	16 sets of 2
Coda	End of vocal to instrumental	24 sets of 2

DANCE NOTE
In every occurrence of the Section A vocal, students should listen for the syncopated figure at the 14th set of 2 on the word *why* and keep counting steadily.

1 Prepare

Background

Why Walk When You Can Fly? is an appropriate song to use for improvising in the traditional dance style called *clogging*. Clogging is an authentic form of American folk dance with roots that reach back to Scottish, Irish, and European heritage. In eighteenth-century England the steel mill workers wore a kind of wooden shoe and this became the shoe of choice for English country dancing. The dancers found them to be very heavy and a hindrance to faster footwork, so they switched to leather, which provided flexibility. To make up for the lost sound of the wooden soles, dancers started the practice of nailing copper pennies to the toes and heels of their shoes.

When clogging is choreographed it is called *precision* style; when improvised, it is called *freestyle.* In freestyle there is usually a leader called a *cuer* who tells the group which of the three basics steps to do.

Warm Up
The students' task will be to invent their own dance sequences, using any combination of steps during both the vocal sections and the instrumental sections. With the three clogging steps shown below, students can explore sequences **in place**, well as **traveling forward, backward,** and **sideward.** Have students practice these steps in place before creating sequences to go with the music.

Clogging Step 1
This is the double-toe clogging step.

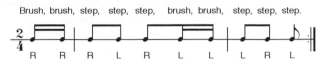

Brush, brush, step, step, step, brush, brush, step, step, step.

Clogging Step 2
This step can be performed in place or traveling to the right, left, or in a circle.

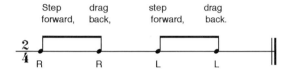

Step   drag   step   drag
forward, back,   forward, back.

Clogging Step 3
Dancers can jump straight forward and back or diagonally to the right and left.

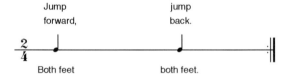

Jump   jump
forward,   back.

Both feet   both feet.

2 Take Action

Formation
Have students stand in random positions all over the room, facing the front.

Create a Clogging Dance
Play the recording of *Why Walk When You Can Fly?* **CD 4-8.** During the solo piano introduction have students demonstrate in movement what they hear in the music. Observe that they move slowly in keeping with the tempo of the music.

SAY Express the free tempo as you wander about the room. Find your own spot before the introduction ends. Be aware of your personal space to avoid collisions.

Section A
When the vocal begins have students perform any combination of clogging steps they design. Instruct them to move **in place**. When the syncopated occurs in the song, have students raise their arms in a flying position and pause briefly.

Section B

Students improvise traveling sequences of clogging steps forward, diagonally, and backward while continuing to be aware of other dancers. Invite them to travel only during the instrumental sections.

Perform as described above, repeating Sections A and B until the Coda.

Coda

Students alternate in-place clogging and traveling clogging sequences to the end of the song.

Freestyle Clogging Dance

Invite individual volunteers to be *cuers* for the dance. Depending on the number of volunteers assign one to lead the dancing for Section A, one to lead Section B, one to lead the Coda. If you have more than three volunteers, have them take turns leading when the sections repeat.

Cuers clog for 2 sets of 2 and the class repeats what the cuers do. Continue to the end of the song.

3 Reflect

Discussion

Have students stand in a circle facing the center. Invite them to share what it was like for them to experience clogging. At the end of the sharing have each student improvise a short clogging "sentence" that says "Thank you. I had a good time today."

———————————

1 Dance by Ear

LESSON AT A GLANCE

Movement Skill Objective Create an interpretive dance based on the patterns and instrumental timbres in a piece of contemporary music

5–8 Dance Standard 2a Clearly demonstrate the principles of contrast and transition

Physical Education Standard 1 Demonstrate competency in motor skills

MATERIALS

- *Daphne of the Dunes*
  Teacher's Edition, Gr. 8, p. D-29 **CD 9-5**
- Props: scarves, streamers, sponge balls, hoops, and so on
- Costumes: uniform clothing, such as jeans, hats, gloves, and so on

DANCE NOTE

For a performance piece, encourage students to think in terms of color and design as they develop the choreography, using props that are common in the classroom, music room, or gym.

DANCE COUNT SEQUENCE

Count straight through each section at a moderate tempo. The counting is not in a particular meter but is for marking time, 1-2-3-4-5-6, and so on, until the next instrument enters or a musical event occurs.

Section	Music Cue	Count
Section A	Fast high and bass xylophones	1–15
Section B	High glass bells, fast xylophones	16–27
Section C	Dry fast xylophones	28–38
Section D	Dry fast metal tones enter, others continue	39–62
Section E	Slow cloud chamber bowls, fast high xylophones	63–82
Section F	Fast xylophones, rhythmic xylophones	83–102
Section G	Fast bass xylophones	103–110
Section H	Slow vibrating bells, fast xylophone	111–131
Section I	Dry chunky bass xylophone, others re-enter and continue	132–174
Section J	Wind chimes enter, fast xylophone continues	175–212

1 Prepare

Warm Up

While students are seated around the room, play the recording of *Daphne of the Dunes* **CD 9-5**. Have them listen for the various instruments as they enter and exit the music. Invite each student to focus on one instrument and begin to isolate its pattern and character. Play the recording again and have students interpret their chosen instruments' patterns.

2 Take Action

Formation

Have students identify their chosen instruments by name (see Dance Count Sequence). Sort the class by music Sections A through J and assign students to those groups based on the instruments they chose to inspire their movements. Each music section will now have a dance ensemble.

Movement Ideas

The following movement ideas are intended as launching pads to creativity. Demonstrate your own interpretation of the movements and have students imitate you. Students should then invent their own moves.

- **Fast High and Low Xylophones**—Form a walk with very fast feet, snaking around the other groups and freezing when their music stops or lie down on their backs, moving their feet rapidly.

- **High Glass Bells**—In movement or in stationar poses outline space by accentuating each occurrence of the bell sound, sustaining the movement while the sound sustains. Students can stand in clusters or in a line and work together.

- **Dry Fast Xylophones**—Rapid and separated steps and gestures.

- **Dry Fast Metal Tones**—In ensemble with dr xylophones, moving in contrary motion.

- **Slow Cloud Chamber Bowls**—Floating movements like a kite on the wind.

- **Rhythmic Xylophones**—Jumping and hopping motions that accentuate the rhythm of the instrument.

- **Slow Vibrating Bells**—Very large movements to *sound* the bells and, while floating on the sustained sound, invent a way to sparkle and vibrate with fingers or small head motions.

- **Dry Chunky Bass Xylophone**—Sharp and angular motions, using shoulders, hips, knees, head, and arms, following the up and down contour of the sounds.

- **Wind Chimes**—Whirling movements.

Create a Dance Sequence

Instruct each group to transfer the finger and hand movements they created during the Warm Up to the whole body and then expand on them. Let the groups know that

- Movements can now become locomotor if desired.
- The members of each section need to understand how to listen for their own music cues and how to count in order to coordinate with the music.
- When two or more "instruments" are moving simultaneously, the movements should be contrasting so that they can be distinguished one from the other.
- They should create a section-ender movement so that the transitions between sections are clear and smooth.

Perform the Dance

Invite students to use props (see Materials) and/or costumes if they will perform their dance in public. After the student groups have established how they will move together in ensemble during their own sections of the music, have them take their places in the room (or on stage). Play the recording and have the class perform the dance accompanied by the music. Observe whether each section has followed the above criteria.

3 Reflect

Discussion

Sitting in a circle facing the center, invite students to share about the experience of using contemporary music to create a dance sequence.

ASK How did your experience of the music change from the beginning of the lesson to the end? (Allow for open discussion. Students may not have liked the music at first and may have grown to appreciate it in the process of creating a dance to go with it.)

---

3 Sports on the Move

LESSON AT A GLANCE

Movement Skill Objective Create specific movement sequences based on defined sports images

5–8 Dance Standard 1g Demonstrate accurate memorization and reproduction of movement sequences

Physical Education Standard 1 Demonstrate competency in motor skills

MATERIALS

- *Good Vibrations* Teacher's Edition, Gr. 8, p. E-28   **CD 10-2**

DANCE COUNT SEQUENCE

Music Cue/Lyrics	CD Counter
I, I love the…	0:00–0:26
I'm thinking of …	0:26–0:51
Close my eyes…	0:51–1:16
I'm thinking of…	1:16–1:42
Excitations–'tations	1:42–2:14
Gonna' keep those…	2:14–2:57
Good, good, good…	2:57–3:13
Do-de-do-de-do…	3:13–3:27
Coda—instrumental	3:27–3:36

1 Prepare

Warm Up

Working silently and in **slow motion**, have students create sports movements-snow skiing, dribbling a basketball, roller skating, surfing, swimming, figure skating, or kicking a soccer ball. Have students exaggerate their moves, especially when things go wrong.

2 Take Action

Create a Sports Dance

Have students work individually and invent movement sequences for the sports activities above. Play **CD 10-2**. Help students notice the sections of the music.

Have students determine sports actions to perform with each section of the music. Some of these, such as skiing and surfing, will be **stationary.** Provide prompts to help students think about their movements, such as "Work the twists and turns of the knees" or "What is the difference between skiing and surfing?"

Other sports movements might be **locomotor** movements. Provide prompts that help students think about appropriate variations for these sports, such as "Old-time figure skaters used to carve in the ice, as well as perform spins and jumps" or "Show how your sport ends-if you take a spill, move in slow motion. If you win a race or game, show how you feel."

Have students implement different sports action sequences with each section of the music. Remind them not to interact with or touch other movers.

3 Reflect

Discussion

Lead a discussion about sports movements. Discuss how technology may have changed a person's ability to engage in different sports.

Music Index